Long Term Care

Customer Service

Instructor's Guide

2nd Edition

Evidenced-Based Training for Skilled Nursing Homes, Assisted Living Facilities and Anyone Working With the Elderly

MT

TO AMY AND MAYA

11/18/15

Table of Contents

Chapter 1
Fundamentals of Customer Service

Module 1

Module 2

Module 3

Module 4

Chapter 2
Managing Customer Care

Chapter 3
Listening Skills

Module 2

Module 3

Chapter 4
Creating Rapport

Module 1

Module 2

Chapter 5
Managing Stress

Chapter 6
Resolving Conflict

ACKNOWLEDGMENTS

Many thanks are due to a handful of generous individuals who contributed to the creation of *Long Term Care Customer Service*:

- Ronnie Barrera
- Theric Brown
- Mark Cooley
- Jay Duquette
- Scott Haile
- Hector Leguillow
- Dr. Dennis Lind
- Jody Montreal
- Darlene Nakayama
- Dr. Jeff Rebarcek
- Andy Tomlinson

How To Use This Instructor's Guide

A customer is more than someone who buys a product or service. They are someone with a set of expectations that the product or service purchased will satisfy its promise.

In a long term care facility your staff members come into daily contact with people who have high expectations for service. Whether they are co-workers, managers or residents your front line staff should consider all of them their customers.

The lessons participants will find in their *Long Term Care Customer Service* Resource Guides – and the effort they put into learning and applying those lessons – will help them improve how they manage themselves and others.

There are three training delivery options for this material and the recommended companion DVD *Long Term Care Customer Service*:

- Instructor-led: a staff member leads participants through the lessons.
- Self-directed: participants work individually on the lessons, quizzes or exercises you provide them.
- Team-directed: participants work in small teams and collaborate on the learning objectives, but take the quizzes individually.

Each chapter of *Long Term Care Customer Service* is divided into learning modules which are each comprised of specific learning objectives. Each module is separated into sections which are approximately 15 minutes in length. The suggested timing to complete each section is based on whether you choose instructor-led or team-directed training delivery. Self-directed learning may require a shorter training period.

At the end of each module there are quiz questions which cover its learning objectives. Each chapter also contains role plays or other learning exercises.

I believe the skills your staff will acquire from *Long Term Care Customer Service* will help them grow personally and professionally. And that growth will be reflected in the quality of care they provide your residents.

All the best,
Rob Anderson
Prima Lux Publishing
primaluxpublishing@yahoo.com

Chapter 1

Fundamentals of Customer Service
Instructor's Guide

Fundamentals of Customer Service is divided into 4 learning modules each with multiple sections. Each module includes a quiz which reviews its learning objectives. A learning exercise can also be found at the end of the chapter.

A nurturing environment for residents and their families is built upon a foundation of excellent customer service.

Learning Objectives

Chapter 1 - Module 1

At the end of this module participants will be able to:

- Identify The Three Circles of Customer Service Success and how they related to each other.

- Describe the types of customers found in a Long Term Care environment.

- Define how customer service applies in Long Term Care.

Participant Resource Guide Page Number: 15

The Three Circles of Customer Service Success

Success as a customer service provider requires that you develop three interlocking sets of skills:

- One skill involves managing yourself which is very helpful when dealing with difficult customers.

- Managing the interaction requires that you move smoothly through the steps to help the customer and end on a positive note.

- A third skill set helps you manage the customer by building rapport and delivering the desired service efficiently.

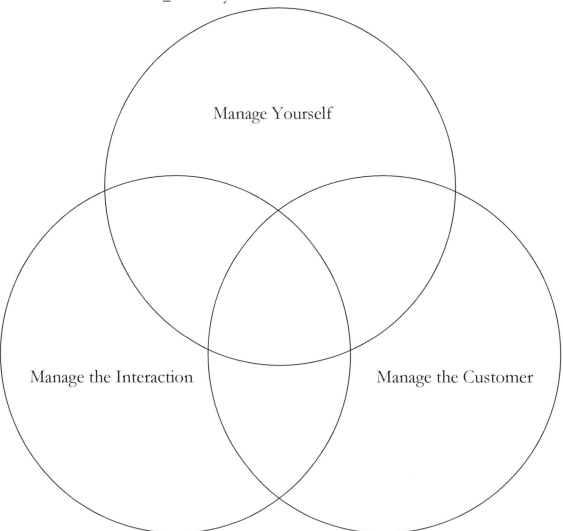

If you want to stand out as a customer service provider you should continually develop your skills in all three areas.

Instructor's Notes

Who Are the Customers Found In a Skilled Nursing or Assisted Living Facility?

- It would be useful at this point to let participants know that residents at your facility are not being compared to a customer at a retail outlet. Residents are referred to as customers only to change the context in which they may be considered (a person to be served). In doing so participants may shift their perspectives to a customer-centered mindset.

- Define and discuss the types of customers found in a long term care environment:

    o A resident

    o A family member of an existing resident

    o A prospective resident

    o A co-worker

    o A referral source such as a physician

    o A volunteer

    o A vendor

- Discuss why each of these people are considered customers.

Approximate Time: 15 minutes

Participant Resource Guide Page Number: 17

Who Are the Customers Found In a
Skilled Nursing or Assisted Living Facility?

The most obvious answer is someone who receives service from you directly like a resident.

But it can also be someone who *indirectly* receives the benefit of your service such as a family member.

o   But what about a prospective resident and their family?

o   Or a referral source such as a physician?

o   What about your co-workers? How do you think the relationship with your colleagues will change if you treat them like your customers?

In other words a customer could be anyone who you interact with every day.

So shouldn't you treat everyone in the spirit of service?

Instructor's Notes

What Exactly Is Customer Service And How Does It Apply To Long Term Care?

- Review and discuss the definition of customer service.
- Discuss the goals of customer service using the acronym **MEL**:
    - o **M**eet, then exceed, the customer's expectations.
    - o **E**ngage the customer with a positive, helpful attitude.
    - o **L**eave the customer satisfied.

Approximate Time: 15 minutes

Participant Resource Guide Page Number: 18

What Exactly Is Customer Service And
How Does It Apply To Long Term Care?

Customer service is the method you use to "deliver" your service to the customer...

but more importantly how you treat the customer in the process.

As a general rule you should not only agree to do what a customer asks, but deliver more. For example, if a resident asks you for a blanket, bring two.

Keep this in mind: If you set out to *do* more than you're asked you'll often *receive* more than you expect.

When setting your goals for delivering exceptional customer service just remember **MEL**:

- **M**eet, then exceed, the customer's expectations.
- **E**ngage the customer with a positive, helpful attitude.
- **L**eave the customer satisfied.

Quiz Questions
Chapter 1 - Module 1

1. What are The Three Circles of Customer Service Success?

   a. *Manage Yourself*

   b. *Manage the Interaction*

   c. *Manage the Customer*

2. Name three types of customers you come in contact with at your facility?

   a. *Residents*

   b. *Co-workers*

   c. *Resident's family members*

3. What are some common goals for customer service delivery (use **MEL** to provide your answer)?

   a. *Meet, then exceed, the customer's expectations.*

   b. *Engage the customer with a positive, helpful attitude.*

   c. *Leave the customer satisfied.*

Approximate Time: 10 minutes

Participant Resource Guide Page Number: 19

Learning Objectives

Chapter 1 - Module 2

At the end of this module participants will be able to:

- Understand the importance of excellent customer service to your community.

- Identify customer touchpoints.

- Recognize how your appearance can affect customer service delivery.

Participant Resource Guide Page Number: 20

What Are the Benefits of Great Customer Service?

- Happier residents and employees.

- Less turnover for both.

- More referrals.

- Residents will be more forgiving if a good relationship is in place with caregivers. For example, complaints are often resolved quickly if great customer service practices are being applied.

- Discuss customer touchpoints. Each time we interact with a customer we have an impact on how they perceive us.

- Customer touchpoints include:

  o Pleasantly greeting a vendor or co-worker.

  o Helping a resident pick something up.

  o Assisting a nurse's aide or housekeeper unasked.

  o Staying late to finish a task (provided that task will affect someone other than just you).

  o Greeting a visitor in the facility's parking lot.

Approximate Time: 15 minutes

Participant Resource Guide Page Numbers: 21-22

What Are the Benefits of Great Customer Service?

In Chapter One you learned what customer service is and who your customers are. But how does providing great customer service benefit the people you work with and the residents you care for?

Here is a simple formula:

Fewer Problems = Less Friction = Happier Residents And Staff

When you apply what you learn in this course you may find:

- Happier residents and co-workers.
- Less turnover for both.
- More referrals.

You may also find that your customers will be more forgiving of mistakes if you have a good relationship with them.

Customer Touchpoints

Each time you interact with a customer you impact how they perceive the care you provide and your facility as a whole.

Each of these customer interactions, no matter how trivial, is called a touchpoint. A touchpoint results in either a good or bad impression.

For example, when you greet a visitor – that's a touchpoint.

When you *don't* say good morning as you enter a resident's room – that's a touchpoint and a missed opportunity.

When you comfort a family member – that's a compassionate and powerful touchpoint.

List three examples of positive touch points and three examples of negative touch points you have either experienced or witnessed recently at your facility.

_____

_____

_____

_____

_____

_____

Instructor's Notes

Consistently Applying Great Customer Service Has Other Benefits

- Discuss the importance of preventing litigation at your facility including costs, negative ratings, etc.

- Facilitate a discussion about appearance using your facility's' dress code as the basis. Bear in mind that some participants may be uncomfortable discussing their wardrobe and grooming habits publicly.

Approximate Time: 15 minutes

Participant Resource Guide Page Number: 23

Consistently Applying Great Customer Service Has Other Benefits

Great customer service creates an advantage over the competition

Often the only differences between one long term care facility and another is how a potential resident is greeted upon arrival, the friendliness of their tour guide and the warmth of the staff members the visitor interacts with.

Customer service may reduce the risk of lawsuit

Reducing lawsuits may be achieved by regularly asking what issues, needs or questions residents may have then following up on their concerns.

Being thoughtful, honest and dedicated to finding solutions can keep tempers – and potential lawsuits – at bay.

Your appearance matters for delivering excellent customer service

Why would your choice of outfit, makeup or jewelry make a difference when you're trying to address a complaint or understand a resident's problem?

Your appearance is the first thing people notice and it signals to them if you are professional and capable. Appropriate dress and grooming inspires confidence in those you serve.

What are your facility's standards for attire, jewelry and makeup? What about piercings and body art?

_____

_____

_____

Quiz Questions

Chapter 1 - Module 2

1. Name 3 benefits great customer service provides to your community.

    a. *Happier residents and employees.*

    b. *Less turnover for both.*

    c. *Fewer complaints – people are more forgiving if a good relationship is in place with caregivers.*

2. List 3 customer touchpoints.

    a. *Pleasantly greeting a vendor or co-worker.*

    b. *Assisting a co-worker unasked.*

    c. *Greeting a visitor in your facility's parking lot.*

3. List 3 ways you meet your facility's dress code.

    a. *My clothes are free of stains and tears and are ironed.*

    b. *My makeup is appropriate for a professional environment.*

    c. *My name tag is displayed in the required location.*

Approximate Time: 15 minutes

Participant Resource Guide Page Number: 24

Learning Objectives

Chapter 1 - Module 3

At the end of this module participants will be able to:

- Recognize how improving meal service can have a positive effect.

- Understand the impact of a dissatisfied customer.

- Explain the importance of attitude in being an effective Customer Service Provider.

Participant Resource Guide Page Number: 25

Instructor's Notes

Satisfying Customers One Meal at a Time

- Facilitate a discussion about Daniel's story with a focus on how your facility can improve meal service.

- Ask participants what special touches they might "bring to the table" to improve meal service.

  - o Some ideas might include:

    - ▪ Bussing tables faster so diners have shorter waits.

    - ▪ Preparing meals per a resident's request including pre-cutting certain foods to make eating easier and safer.

    - ▪ Playing soft music in the background.

    - ▪ Discussing the meal options with each resident.

Approximate Time: 15 minutes

Participant Resource Guide Page Number: 26

Satisfying Customers One Meal at a Time

Mealtime for many residents is the only time they socialize, making the dining experience a very important customer touchpoint.

Isn't great service one of the reasons we frequent a restaurant?

Daniel is a nursing facility administrator who felt that mealtimes needed to better reflect the importance that residents placed on that part of their day.

So he recommended that staff should:

- **Greet diners** at the door, escort them to their tables and hold their chairs.

- **Note complaints and compliments.**

- **Service tables quickly** by refreshing water glasses and clearing dishes.

- **Think about how to continue to improve the dining experience.**

Everyone was delighted with the changes because it lifted the mood at meal time, engaged residents to share their thoughts about service…and cost nothing to implement.

What is one change you would suggest to make meal times more enjoyable for residents at your facility?

_____

_____

_____

Instructor's Notes

Customer Dissatisfaction

- Have participants share both good and bad customer service experiences.
  - o Discuss the outcome of bad customer service experiences that the participants identified. How many of them actually complained? How many simply stopped doing business with the organization?

- Determine if most participants find it easier to recall bad customer service experiences over good ones. Facilitate a discussion on why this might occur.

- Ask participants what they are more likely to talk about with others: a good or bad customer service experience. What do they hear about more often from friends and family?

Approximate Time: 15 minutes

Participant Resource Guide Page Number: 27

Customer Dissatisfaction

So far we've discussed how customer service can have a positive effect on the people you serve.

But what happens when a customer is not satisfied?

A recent study concluded that:

- 5% of complaints are made directly to nursing home management.

- 45% of residents complain only to front line staff.

- **50% of residents don't complain at all**.

While that may make your day flow a little smoother those unknown complaints will be uncovered during yearly surveys and when speaking with resident's families.

Improving customer service is accomplished largely by responding to customer complaints *every day*.

Attitude

- Facilitate a discussion about attitude.
    - o Consider the different ways that we use the term. (Regarding someone who is outspoken or assertive -- "He's got an attitude". Or someone who is being rebellious or offensive in some way – "Don't give me that attitude".)
    - o Ask participants how they can tell when a resident or co-worker is "giving them an attitude". Their responses should include how the person acts and that their actions imply an opinion about someone or something.
- Ask participants how they think their attitude impacts:
    - o Residents
    - o Co-workers
    - o Supervisors

Approximate Time: 15 minutes

Participant Resource Guide Page Number: 28

Attitude

How does your attitude affect your performance on the job and impact those around you?

Your attitude has two important parts:

- o **How you feel about something or someone.**

- o **How you behave in a situation.**
  - Keep in mind your behavior is a mirror of your attitude.

Let's say you didn't get much sleep the night before, spilled coffee on your scrubs and were late for work. When you show up you're irritable and short-tempered.

What kind of impact do you think your bad mood might have on the quality of service you provide your customers?

What steps would you take to improve your attitude?

_____

_____

_____

Quiz Questions

Chapter 1 - Module 3

1. What are some ways you can improve your facility's meal service?

   a. Bussing tables faster so diners have shorter waits.

   b. Preparing meals per a resident's request including pre-cutting certain foods to make eating easier and safer.

   c. Playing soft music in the background.

   d. Discussing the meal options with each resident.

2. According to a study, what percentage of residents complain about bad customer service?

   25%   **50%**   10% 90%

3. Name the two components of your attitude.

   a. Your general state of mind about something or someone (how you feel).

   b. How you come across in a situation (how you behave).

Approximate Time: 15 minutes

Participant Resource Guide Page Number: 29

Learning Objectives

Chapter 1 - Module 4

At the end of this module participants will be able to:

- Identify the behaviors of the Friendly and Authoritative Attitudes.

- Use both the Credible and Approachable Voices.

Participant Resource Guide Page Number: 30

Instructor's Notes

Friendly Attitude

- Facilitate a discussion on the importance of having a friendly attitude as a Customer Service Provider. Note that the provider is expected to be friendly even when the customer is not. Most customers, even those that are upset, tend to eventually trust and connect with someone being genuine, warm and positive.

    o Ask participants to contribute their ideas about what "being friendly" means to them.

- Demonstrate the approachable voice:

    o Be sure to smile when you speak.

    o Move your head up and down gently as you modulate your voice tone.

- Have participants practice the approachable voice using the simple sentences below.

    o How are you today?

    o How can I help you?

    o Did you enjoy this morning's activities?

- Facilitate a discussion on when an approachable voice is useful and when it is not.

Approximate Time: 15 minutes

Participant Resource Guide Page Number: 31

Friendly Attitude

All of us desire a genuine, friendly connection with others whether we're customers or not.

Not surprisingly then a *friendly attitude* is a basic requirement for all customer service positions and has two important parts:

How you feel, meaning:

- **You generally like people.**

- **And are happy to be working with a customer.**

How you act, that is you:

- **Speak with a smile on your face and in your voice.**

- **Express appreciation and offer encouragement to the customer.**

- **Invite questions and input.**

- **Use the "approachable" voice.**

When you want to sound open and inviting speak with an upward inflection at the end of the sentence.

Some examples include:

- Can I help you?

- Did you enjoy this morning's activities?

Be careful overusing this form of speech because it can create the perception that you lack confidence.

Instructor's Notes

Authoritative Attitude

- Facilitate a discussion on the importance of acting with authority as a Customer Service Provider.
    - o Ask participants to contribute their ideas about what "acting with authority" means to them.
- Demonstrate the credible voice.
    - o Be sure to maintain a straight face with only a slight smile.
    - o Keep your head relatively still as you speak in an even tone and then drop your head slightly at the downward inflection.
- Have participants practice the credible voice using the simple sentences below.
    - o I can help you with that.
    - o Our staff nurse can answer your questions.
    - o I know exactly where to get that information.
- Facilitate a discussion on when a credible voice is useful and when it is not.

Approximate Time: 15 minutes

Participant Resource Guide Page Number: 32

Authoritative Attitude

Most customers are sensitive to any signal that a Customer Service Provider can't help them.

You can reassure your customers by acting with authority.

The *authoritative attitude* also has two basic components:

How you feel, that is:

- **You have a genuine desire to help the customer.**

- **You're confident in your knowledge and skills.**

How you act. You...

- **Reassure the customer that you can help.**

- **Tell them you will hold yourself accountable.**

- **Use the "credible" voice.**

When you want to sound decisive and confident speak with a calm, steady voice using a downward inflection at the end of the sentence.

Some examples include:

- I can help you with that.

- I know exactly where to get that information.

Overuse of the credible voice can give the impression that you are not interested in the customer's input.

Quiz Questions

Chapter 1 - Module 4

1. What are four actions associated with friendliness?

    a. *Speaking with a smile in your voice and responding warmly to the customer's input.*

    b. *Expressing appreciation to the customer.*

    c. *Offering encouraging remarks to the customer.*

    d. *Inviting customer questions and input at appropriate times.*

2. What are three actions associated with authority?

    a. *Stating that you* can *help the customer.*

    b. *Explaining how you* will *help the customer.*

    c. *Reassuring the customer.*

3. Make diagrams of the credible voice pattern and the approachable voice pattern.

    a. Approachable Voice:

    b. Credible Voice:

Approximate Time: 15 minutes

Participant Resource Guide Page Number: 33

Instructor's Notes

Learning Exercise: Letter from a Resident

Goal:

> To identify, through a 3rd person perspective, how good customer service positively affects residents.

Materials:

> Participants may use the worksheet "Letter from a Resident" found on page 34 in their Resource Guide.

Approximate Time:

> 30 minutes

Instructions:

- Participants write a fictional letter from a resident to themselves that highlights how their attitude, service and compassion have had a positive impact on the resident's life.

- When this exercise is complete participants can read their letters to the group.

Learning Exercise: Letter from a Resident

Instructions: Using the space below write a fictional letter from a resident to yourself that highlights how your attitude, your service and your compassion have had a positive impact on their life.

Chapter 2

Managing Customer Care
Instructor's Guide

Managing Customer Care is divided into 2 learning modules each with multiple sections. Each module includes a quiz which reviews its learning objectives. A learning exercise can also be found within the chapter.

> **Knowing what to say and do as a professional customer service provider will make working with customers more effective and fulfilling.**

Learning Objectives

Chapter 2 - Module 1

At the end of this module participants will be able to:

- Identify the Seven Steps For Helping a Customer.

- Apply the Seven Steps to a variety of customer situations.

Participant Resource Guide Page Number: 35

The Three Circles of Customer Service Success

Chapter 2 Managing Customer Care reviews some of the skill sets required for managing the interaction with a customer. This is one of The Three Circles of CS Success that you must understand to be effective as a customer service provider.

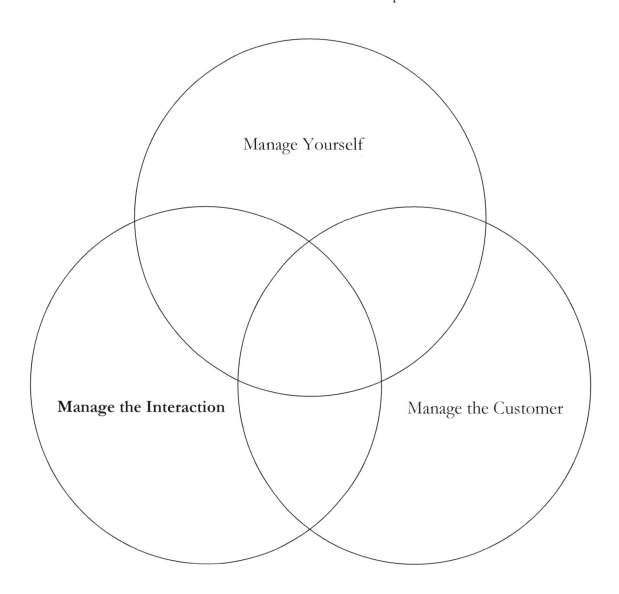

Manage the Interaction

You manage a customer interaction by:

- Holding yourself responsible for the customer's satisfaction.

- Understanding the steps of an interaction and keeping track of where you are in the process.

- Finishing your conversation with the customer on a positive note.

Participant Resource Guide Page Number: 36

Instructor's Notes

The Seven Steps for Helping a Customer

- Effective customer service providers prepare themselves mentally before they speak with a customer.

- Lead a discussion on the Seven Steps.
    - The first two steps reflect two of the Elements of Effective Communication: "Picture Your Goal" and "Manage Your Attitude" (see Instructor's Guide Chapter 4 "Creating Rapport" page 103).

- Ask participants to define a positive goal for helping a customer. Examples include: meeting, then exceeding, customer expectations; ending the conversation positively; building rapport with the customer.

- Discuss the importance of personalizing the service. Ask participants to revisit times when they received good service. What did the customer service provider do to personalize the service for them? How did personalization make them feel as customers? Examples may include being called by name, feeling respected, etc.

- Have participants rehearse the line: "I can help you with that." This should be spoken warmly using the "Approachable Voice" (see Instructor's Guide Chapter 1 "Fundamentals of Customer Service", page 38) which has an upward inflection at the end of the sentence. Offer variations of the statement above. Examples include: "It is my pleasure to help you with that"; "I'd be happy to take care of that for you"; etc.

- Mention that moving smoothly between the steps of a customer interaction demonstrates professionalism and helps maintain rapport.

Approximate Time: 30 minutes

Participant Resource Guide Page Numbers: 37-38

The Seven Steps for Helping a Customer

Follow the steps below and most customer interactions will flow more smoothly:

1. Remember that your goal is to meet, then exceed, your customer's expectations.

- Additional goals include: ending the conversation positively and building rapport with the customer.

2. Create a focused state of mind before speaking with your customer.

- One way to accomplish this is picture yourself on a dark stage. Now imagine a spot light suddenly shining on you. That light is your customer's expectation of quality service.

- Consider this: Preparation is the difference between just a spotlight above you and headlights coming at you.

3. Greet the customer with a positive and enthusiastic tone.

- You only have one chance to make a first impression. Offer your greeting "I can help you with that" with the approachable voice and a smile.

4. Gather all the necessary information to find out what the customer wants.

- This requires asking questions and using effective listening skills.

- A customer service provider is like a limo driver. Your job is to comfortably take the customer where they want to go.

5. Deliver the desired service efficiently and courteously.

- **"Own" the service delivery.** When you decide to help a customer you accept responsibility for their satisfaction and must hold yourself accountable for delivering.

- **Acknowledge the customer's situation.** Are they upset? Tense? Tired? Frustrated?

- **Keep the customer informed.** You may have look up information or speak to a supervisor, but let the customer know what you're doing. This will help them relax.

- **Ask permission.**

o Would your customer prefer to wait, be put on hold or have you call back?

o If you need to transfer a call here are the steps to follow:

- Contact your co-worker to explain the situation.

- Connect the caller and co-worker then introduce them.

- Make a supportive comment about the co-worker's ability to handle the call.

- Thank the customer and hang up.

- **Provide explanations.** If you must ask a customer for personal information offer a brief reason for doing so.

- **Follow-through on promises.** Customers are sensitive to any words or phrases that may be taken as promises. If you do make a promise be sure to fulfill it or hold yourself responsible if you don't.

- **Make requests, not demands.** For instance, ask the customer "May I have your room number?" rather than "Give me your room number."

6. Bring the conversation to a positive close.

- Confirm that the service the customer wanted was delivered to their satisfaction.

- Once the customer is satisfied ask if there are any other issues to address.

7. Prepare for the next customer.

- Take a series of slow and deep breaths to release any tension.

Instructor's Notes

Learning Exercise: Applying the Seven Steps for Helping a Customer

Goal:

Provide participants the opportunity to practice the guidelines they have learned.

Materials:

Applying the Seven Steps for Helping a Customer worksheet found in the participant's Resource Guide on page 39.

Approximate Time:

30 minutes

Instructions:

- Break participants into groups of two with one person playing the "Staff Member" and one the "Resident". Assign participants one of the three scenarios found on the worksheet. You can also use an actual scenario from your facility as the basis for one of the role plays.

- After the role plays conclude, record the key words and phrases used by the "Staff Members" which successfully guided their interactions with the "Residents".

Learning Exercise: Applying the Seven Steps for Helping a Customer

Using the following scenarios as guidelines, create role-plays between a "Staff Member" and a "Resident". You may use the space below each scenario for making notes.

A very demanding resident, Mr. Jernell, walks up to you asking what time his dentist appointment is, even though you've told him twice before. You are in the middle of assisting another staff member when he asks you. **What do you say to Mr. Jernell? To your co-worker?**

_____

_____

Mrs. Torres is upset about the behavior of another resident who she believes is harassing her. Because she has made this complaint previously you've spoken to the accused resident who denies any problem exists. Now Mrs. Torres wants to speak with the administrator. **How should you handle this situation?**

_____

_____

Miss Li complains that her necklace, a family heirloom, is missing and thinks it may have accidentally dropped into her room's wastebasket the night before. After checking the room and wastebasket, which was emptied the previous night, you decide to contact the night and maintenance supervisors to learn if they've found the jewelry. Miss Li is very worried and wants to stay with you until her property is found. **How do you reassure Miss Li that you will get back to her when you receive a report from the two staff members? How will you make sure that you don't forget to follow up?**

_____

_____

Seven Steps for Helping a Customer (Outline)

(You may remove this page from your workbook and keep it near your workstation as a reminder)

Before the
conversation

1. Remember that your goal is to meet, then exceed, a customer's expectations.

2. Create a focused state of mind before speaking with the customer.

3. Greet the customer with a positive and enthusiastic tone.

During the
conversation

4. Gather necessary information to find out what the customer wants.

5. Deliver the desired service efficiently and courteously.

After the
conversation

6. Bring the conversation to a positive close.

7. Prepare for the next customer.

Quiz Questions

Chapter 2 - Module 1

1. What are the Seven Steps for Helping a Customer?

   a. Remember that your goal is to <u>meet</u>, then <u>exceed,</u> a customer's expectations.

   b. Create a <u>focused</u> state of mind before speaking with the customer.

   c. Greet the customer with a <u>positive</u> and <u>enthusiastic</u> tone.

   d. Gather all the <u>necessary</u> information to find out what the customer wants.

   e. Deliver the desired service <u>efficiently</u> and <u>courteously.</u>

   f. Bring the conversation to a <u>positive</u> close.

   g. <u>Prepare</u> for the next customer.

2. What are the 4 steps to transfer a call?

   a. Contact the <u>co-worker</u> to explain the situation.

   b. Connect the caller and co-worker then <u>introduce</u> them.

   c. Make a <u>supportive</u> comment about the co-worker's ability to handle the call.

   d. Thank the customer and <u>hang-up.</u>

3. What should you do if you are unable to fulfill a promise made to a customer?

   <u>Immediately apologize, hold yourself responsible and promise to fulfill the customer's request as soon as possible.</u>

4. What does it mean to own the service delivery?

   <u>Accept responsibility for a customer's satisfaction and hold yourself accountable for delivering it.</u>

Approximate Time: 15 minutes

Participant Resource Guide Page Number: 41

Learning Objectives

Chapter 2 - Module 2

At the end of this module participants will be able to:

- Employ the "Can-Do Attitude".

- Avoid using "Killer Words And Phrases" when working with a customer.

Participant Resource Guide Page Number: 42

Instructor's Notes

"Can-Do Attitude"

- Lead a discussion on positive communication emphasizing the "Can-Do Attitude".

- Note how the "Can-Do Attitude" involves a number of skill sets including:
  o Listening skills
  o Rapport skills
  o Communication skills

Approximate Time: 15 minutes

Participant Resource Guide Page Number: 43

"Can-Do Attitude"

Your customers want your time and attention. Fail to make the effort they require and you'll have an angry customer.

This is why the "Can-Do Attitude" is so important. It allows you to send the message that you will help the customer or find someone who can.

The "Can-Do Attitude" is built upon these important skills:

1. Creating Rapport – we'll learn more about rapport building in Chapter 4.

- Try to find shared interests to talk about.

- Respond to the customer's emotional state by maintaining your composure and offering empathy.

2. Non-verbal communication

- Use open and approachable body language and good eye contact.

3. Verbal communication

- Tell the customer specifically what you are going to do for them and avoid the use of "Killer Words and Phrases".

Instructor's Notes

"Killer Words and Phrases"

- Lead a discussion on "Killer Words and Phrases". State that they can deliver the message that the customer service provider is *not* committed to helping the customer.

- Have participants share some examples of "Killer Words and Phrases" that they have heard as customers. Ask them how they reacted to those comments.

Approximate Time: 15 minutes

Participant Resource Guide Page Number: 44

"Killer Words and Phrases"

Certain words and phrases may "kill" the connection you have developed with your customer.

For example:

Telling a customer: "I can't..." I won't..." I shouldn't..."

- Instead focus on what you *can* do for them.

Using your resource guide describe what you would say to a resident who needs assistance while you're working with someone else.

_____

_____

Another example is telling a customer that what they said occurred did not happen.

- Instead, empathize with the customer's situation, determine what they want and work toward a solution.

What would you say if a resident tells you the administrator promised her something you know could not be true?

_____

_____

You'll also want to avoid telling a customer that their statement may be valid, but....

- When the word "but" comes *after* something positive and is followed by a negative comment, the "but" cancels the positive and emphasizes the negative.

For example, let's say you tell your coworker: "Thanks for mopping up the spill for me, but you left a puddle under the bed".

**Will your co-worker feel the same appreciation if you hadn't added the criticism?
Circle Yes or No.**

Quiz Questions

Chapter 2 - Module 2

1. A "Can-Do Attitude" is built upon what 3 important skills?

    a. Creating rapport.

    b. Non-verbal communication.

    c. Verbal communication.

2. List three "Killer Words and Phrases" and offer positive alternatives.

Killer Word/Phrase	Positive Alternative
"I can't help you now."	*"I'll be happy to help you in a few minutes."*
"That could not have happened."	*"That sounds like a frustrating experience. Let me verify some information please…"*
"I'd like to help you, but my shift ended five minutes ago."	*"My shift just ended, Mr. Tyler, but I will help you find your glasses once I let my supervisor know I'm still here."*

Approximate Time: 15 Minutes

Participant Resource Guide Page Number: 45

Chapter 3

Listening Skills
Instructor's Guide

Listening Skills is divided into 3 learning modules each with multiple sections. Each module includes a quiz which reviews its learning objectives. Learning exercises are also included in this chapter.

Improving your listening skills will greatly enhance relationships with residents, their families and your co-workers.

Learning Objectives

Chapter 3 - Module 1

At the end of this module participants will be able to:

- Understand that listening is a skill that can be developed.

- Recognize internal and external barriers to listening and learn to overcome them.

- Identify the verbal and nonverbal signals that someone is listening.

Participant Resource Guide Page Number: 46

The Three Circles of Customer Service Success

Chapter 3 Listening Skills reviews some of the skill sets required for managing yourself. This is one of The Three Circles of CS Success that you must understand to be effective as a customer service provider.

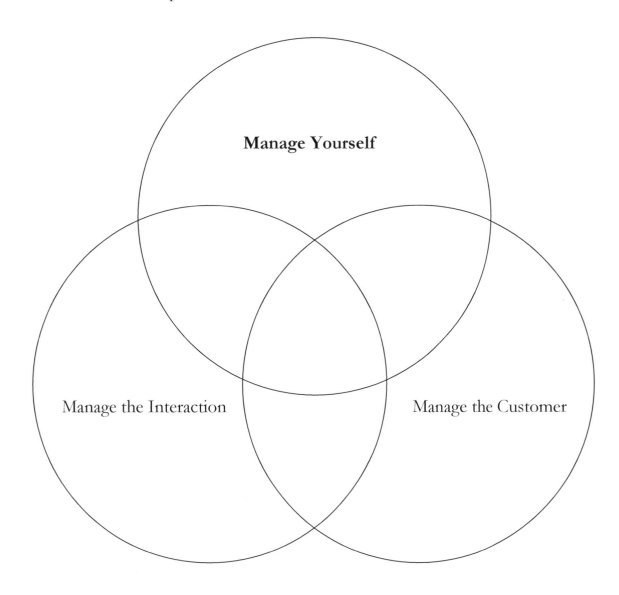

Manage Yourself

You manage yourself by:

- Overcoming any internal barriers to listening.
- Setting an intention to understand what is being said.

Participant Resource Guide Page Number: 47

Instructor's Notes

What is Listening?

- Listening is considered natural so little or no effort is put into learning to listen.

- Ask participants to think about the people they know who they believe are good listeners. What do they think makes these people good listeners? Could it be they:

    o Make great eye contact?

    o Appear to follow what's being said by nodding and saying "mmm-hmm"?

    o Do not make judgments about what's being said?

    o Don't interrupt?

Approximate Time: 15 minutes

Participant Resource Guide Page Number: 48

What is Listening?

Good customer service hinges upon understanding the customer's spoken and unspoken expectations and needs.

There is a difference between hearing and listening. Hearing is a passive process. You'll naturally hear sounds within human range unless there is some impairment.

Listening, however, is an active process. When listening, you focus your attention toward understanding.

Listening skills can be developed when you have:

An Intention to Listen

- You must have the desire to hear and understand what the other person is saying.

A Focused State of Mind

- Your mind must be free of distractions so that you can truly focus on what you're hearing.

A Process for Verifying Meaning

- When appropriate, you should attempt to feedback what's said in order to clarify your understanding. We'll get into more detail on verifying in Module 2.

What do you think makes people great listeners? Do they:

- Maintain eye contact?

- Appear to follow what's being said by nodding and verbalizing?

- Refrain from judging and interrupting?

What are your listening strengths? Weaknesses?

_____

_____

Barriers to Effective Listening

- Facilitate a discussion about specific ways that participants overcome barriers to listening. Their responses may include:

  o Setting the intention to listen to another person.

  o Focusing on the person and what they are saying.

  o Making a conscious effort to set aside any distractions.

  o Redirecting attention to the person and what they are saying when becoming distracted.

- Discuss how elderly residents may have physical impairments such as poor hearing or vision which require:

  o A care giver to speak slowly and clearly and use gestures to better communicate. A quick check of a resident's glasses and hearing aids may also uncover impediments to communication.

  o Sitting with a resident instead of standing over them when speaking. This allows the resident to see and hear better which improves communication.

Approximate Time: 15 minutes

Participant Resource Guide Page Number: 49

Barriers to Effective Listening

One of the most powerful actions you can take to improve your listening skills is to eliminate or overcome common barriers to listening.

Internal Barriers	**External Barriers**
Some internal barriers include: • Thinking of what you'll say next • Illness • Being distracted	Some external barriers include: • The speaker mumbling or not speaking a language you understand • Culture since they have unique modes of expression • Loud music, traffic or other noise in the environment

Remember you can overcome barriers to listening when you:

• Set your intention to listen.

• Focus on what's being said.

• Verify what you've heard.

Some elderly residents may have physical impairments such as poor hearing or vision which require a caregiver to:

• Speak slowly and use gestures. A quick check of a resident's glasses and hearing aids may uncover a problem.

• Sit with a resident when speaking so you can make eye contact.

Instructor's Notes

Verbal and Nonverbal Communication

- Facilitate a discussion about the difference between these two interconnected modes of communication.

- Nonverbal communication includes all of the following cues:
    - Gestures
    - Touch
    - Body Language or Posture
    - Physical Distance
    - Facial Expression
    - Eye Contact
    - Voice Quality
    - Speaking Rate
    - Pitch
    - Volume
    - Intonation

Approximate Time: 15 minutes

Participant Resource Guide Page Number: 50

Verbal and Nonverbal Communication

Think of the words we use every day as bricks loosely stacked together. In order to make our communication fully understood we use nonverbal expressions to "cement" our words into meaningful messages.

For example, let's say you ask a resident: "How are you feeling today?" They respond with "I'm fine", but their body language, depressed tone and lack of eye contact tell you something different.

<u>Verbal Expressions</u>	<u>Nonverbal Expressions</u>
Words	Facial Expressions
Vocalizations (mm-hmm, uh-huh, etc.)	Tone of Voice
	Hand and Body Movement
	Eye Contact
	Posture

Instructor's Notes

Are You Being Listened To?

- Have participants identify indicators (cues) that someone is listening.

  - Some examples of physical cues are touch, gestures, facial expression and eye contact. Auditory cues include utterances such as "uh-huh", "yes", "oh", "hmmm".

- Facilitate a discussion on the results from above. Note that it is a basic human need to be heard and understood. Discuss emotional and behavioral responses when we are *not* being listened to.

- Additional questions to ask include:

  - Are there times when it is not important to be heard? (When talking to oneself or "just babbling").

  - What are the differences between listening cues in person and on the phone?

Approximate Time: 15 minutes

Participant Resource Guide Page Number: 51

Are You Being Listened To?

How do you know when someone is really listening to you? Although there are some common indicators that someone is listening, you may have your own means to determine when you are really being heard.

What signals indicate that someone is listening to you? How do you feel when someone is really listening?

_____

_____

_____

How do you feel when you sense that someone is *not* listening to you?

_____

_____

_____

When beginning a conversation with someone remember what it feels like to be truly listened to and...

Do unto others!

Quiz Questions

Chapter 3 - Module 1

1. What 3 skills are required for effective listening?

    a. *An intention to listen*

    b. *A focused state of mind*

    c. *A process for verifying meaning*

2. List 3 barriers to listening and identify whether the barrier is internal or external.

Possible answers include:

    a. _____ *Traffic noise - External* _____

    b. _____ *Thinking of your response in advance - Internal* _____

    c. _____ *Feeling poorly/illness - Internal* _____

3. How do you know when someone is listening to you?

    Some examples include the listener: touching your hand, having open body language, making encouraging gestures, offering attentive facial expressions and eye contact as well as utterances such as "uh-huh", "yes", "oh", "hmmm".

4. What can you do to improve communication with a resident who is challenged by internal barriers such as poor hearing or eyesight?

    Speak slowly and clearly, sit with them for better eye contact and use gestures to communicate. A quick check of a resident's glasses and hearing aids may also uncover a problem.

Approximate Time: 15 minutes

Participant Resource Guide Page Number: 52

Learning Objectives

Chapter 3 - Module 2

At the end of this module participants will be able to:

- Understand the benefits of listening.

- Apply the required skills to listen actively.

- Identify when and when not to listen actively.

Participant Resource Guide Page Number: 53

Instructor's Notes

Benefits of Listening

- Facilitate a discussion on the benefits of listening.

- Ask participants to give an example of each benefit as it relates to your community.

Approximate Time: 15 minutes

Participant Resource Guide Page Number: 54

Benefits of Listening

Listening is one of a Customer Service Providers most effective tools because:

Listening is a powerful form of acknowledgement.

- Listening is a way of saying "You are important".

Listening creates acceptance.

- It conveys the message that "I'm not judging you."

Listening is the foundation of understanding.

- Since it encourages you to let go of assumptions and seek the speaker's true meaning.

Listening builds stronger relationships.

- The speaker will feel acknowledged, accepted and understood -- and may return the favor.

Listening leads to learning.

- Since it creates openness to other ideas.

Listening minimizes stress.

- Listening carefully reduces miscommunication.

Instructor's Notes

The Skill of Active Listening

- Emphasize the two prime benefits of active listening: increased understanding of the speaker and less miscommunication.

- Discuss the acronym SLANT as it's used as a mnemonic device to remember the basics of active listening:

> **S**it up
>
> **L**ean Forward
>
> **A**ct Interested
>
> **N**od
>
> **T**rack Speaker

Approximate time: 15 minutes

Participant Resource Guide Page Number: 55

The Skill of Active Listening

People who are considered excellent listeners develop the skill of active listening.

- Active listening allows for feedback that ensures you understand a speaker's message.

- Active listening includes all of the signals that you are listening such as eye contact and verbalizations like "uh-huh" and "hmmm".

Remember SLANT when you want to use active listening:

Sit up

Lean Forward

Act Interested

Nod

Track Speaker

Instructor's Notes

When to Use Active Listening

- Facilitate a discussion on when to use active listening and when not to use it.

- When to use it:

    o When accuracy is important

    o With emotional issues (when you want to help someone regain control of themselves)

- When not to use it:

    o During casual conversations

    o With general information when accuracy is not important

- Discuss how to set up active listening with another person.

    o A listener might say to a speaker "I just want to be certain that I understand what you're saying…" then feedback the speaker's message.

Approximate Time: 15 minutes

Participant Resource Guide Page Number: 56

When to Use Active Listening

Active listening is a valuable tool. But like all tools it works best in certain situations.

Active listening is *most* useful:

- When accuracy is important.

- With emotional issues (when you want to help someone regain control of themselves).

Active listening may seem odd unless it is introduced properly. A typical example would be to use the phrase "Just so I understand what you're saying..." then repeat the speaker's message.

You won't need to use active listening during a casual conversation. Wouldn't it be awkward to ask someone "Just so I understand, are you saying you *really* like your cup of coffee?"

Miscommunication can have serious consequences in a Long Term Care environment.

For example, a resident may be experiencing a medical problem, but might be reluctant to say something. You could miss an opportunity to assist if you're *not* looking for nonverbal signals and using active listening.

Instructor's Notes

Learning Exercise: Active Listening

Goal:

This exercise is designed for practicing active listening skills.

Materials:

The page entitled "Active Listening Exercise" which is found in the participant's Resource Guide on page 57.

Approximate Time:

30 minutes

Instructions:

- The purpose of the stem sentence is to start a conversation. After the first round, the listener can paraphrase the speaker, get confirmation and then ask a follow-up question. As the speaker responds to the follow-up question, the listener again uses active listening techniques.

- Form groups of three. One person is the speaker, one is the listener and one is an observer. After each round the participants change roles. The observer's task is to notice what occurs between the speaker and the listener.

- If appropriate, demonstrate the set-up by asking for two volunteers. Play the role of listener.

- Emphasize the importance of keeping the stem sentence completion relatively short with no more than four sentences. This allows the listener to track and paraphrase in manageable portions.

Learning Exercise: Active Listening

Form groups of three for the following exercise. One person is the speaker, one is the listener and one is an observer. Make notes about how the exercise affected you as a speaker and as a listener. As observer, notice what occurs between the speaker and the listener.

The speaker will finish the first stem sentence below while the listener focuses on the message. As listener, nod your head and acknowledge the speaker. As speaker, limit your completion of the stem sentence to four sentences.

When the speaker is finished, the listener briefly restates what the speaker said using an introductory phrase such as "What I hear you saying is…" or "As I understand it, you…" Finish by asking the speaker "Is that right?"

Move on only if the speaker confirms the accuracy of the listener's statement. If not, the speaker should clarify further and the listener should paraphrase again. Continue until the listener receives confirmation that what they are hearing is accurate. Rotate so that each person has a chance to be speaker, listener and observer.

Stem Sentences

    1. If I could change one thing about myself, I would…

    2. I admire people who can…

    3. I would love to have the chance to…

Take time to talk about the exercise after each round. The observer can give feedback to the listener about their focus and recall.

Alternative stem sentences

What I like least about my job is…	My strongest points are…
I get stressed out when…	When I am criticized, I usually…
One thing that really frustrates me is…	The emotion I find most difficult to handle is…

Quiz Questions

Chapter 3 - Module 2

1. List four benefits of listening.

    a. _____ *Encourages openness* _____

    b. _____ *Builds relationships* _____

    c. _____ *Leads to learning* _____

    d. _____ *Minimizes stress* _____

2. What is active listening?

    - *Active listening allows for feedback that ensures you understand a speaker's message.*

    - *Active listening includes all of the signals that you are listening such as eye contact and verbalizations like "uh-huh" and "hmmm".*

3. When should you use active listening? When should you not?

    - When to use it:
        o *When accuracy is important*
        o *With emotional issues (when you want to help someone regain control of themselves)*

    - When not to use it:
        o *During casual conversations*

Approximate Time: 15 minutes

Participant Resource Guide Page Number: 58

Learning Objectives

Chapter 3 - Module 3

At the end of this module participants will be able to:

- Identify the eight reasons why we aren't listening to others.

- Demonstrate how to ask questions.

- Understand the benefits of using both open-ended and closed-ended questions.

Participant Resource Guide Page Number: 59

Instructor's Notes

Seven Reasons Why We Aren't Listening

- Ask participants if they can identify themselves with any of the reasons. If they do, how could they improve their listening skills?

Approximate time: 15 minutes

Participant Resource Guide Page Number: 60

Seven Reasons Why We Aren't Listening

If you want to listen so you really hear what others say make sure you're not:

1. **Mind Reading:** You'll hear little or nothing as you think "What is this person really thinking?"

2. **Rehearsing:** Your mental tryouts for "Here's what I'll say next" tune out the speaker.

3. **Filtering:** Some call this selective listening – hearing only what you want to hear.

4. **Dreaming:** Drifting off during a face-to-face conversation can lead to an embarrassing "What did you say?"

5. **Derailing:** Changing the subject too quickly tells others you're not interested in what they're talking about.

6. **Sparring:** You hear what's said but quickly belittle or discount it.

7. **Placating:** Agreeing with everything you heard just to be nice and avoid conflict does *not* mean you're a good listener.

What type of listener do you think *you* are? (You can choose more than one)

_____

_____

_____

_____

Asking Questions

- Questions are a tool for both gathering information and controlling the interaction.

Approximate Time: 15 minutes

Participant Resource Guide Page Number: 61

Asking Questions

A great way to establish rapport with a resident or co-worker is to ask conversational questions about their hobbies, children or experiences.

At other times you will need to ask direct questions in order to help your customer quickly and efficiently. Here are a few guidelines:

1. Ask politely

- Framing your question softly will set a relaxed tone by using "May I…" or "Could I…"

2. Keep questions simple and to the point such as:

- "May I have your father's name?" or "Are you feeling uncomfortable right now?

3. Provide a reason for a personal question

- Since people value their privacy and may be suspicious tell them why you need their personal information before asking.

Instructor's Notes

Types of Questions

- Review and discuss the two types of questions and facilitate a discussion on when to use each type.

- Describe how the questions can be used to direct the conversation as well as to gather information.

Approximate Time: 15 minutes

Participant Resource Guide Page Number: 62

Types of Questions

There are two types of questions you use every day:

1. Open-ended questions..

…cannot be answered with a "yes, "no," or a simple fact (such as a date).

"How are you feeling this morning?"

> **Open-ended questions
> "open up" the conversation.**

Write an example of an open-ended question you would ask a resident.

---

2. Closed-ended questions...

…are asked to get a yes/no answer or a specific piece of information.

> **Closed-ended questions
> "close in" on a fact.**

Write an example of a closed-ended question you would ask a resident.

Quiz Questions

Chapter 3 - Module 3

1. What are the guidelines for asking questions?

   a. Ask politely
   b. Keep questions simple and to the point
   c. Provide a rationale for any question that is not obvious or is personal

2. What is an open-ended question? Give an example.

   Questions that cannot be answered with "yes, "no," or a simple fact.
   Example: How may I help you?

3. What is a closed-ended question? Give an example.

   Questions used to gather either a yes/no answer or a very specific piece of information.
   Example: Do you need help finding your shoes, Mrs. Barrett?

4. List 7 reasons why we aren't listening to others.

   a. Mind Reading
   b. Rehearsing
   c. Filtering
   d. Dreaming
   e. Derailing
   f. Sparring
   g. Placating

Approximate Time: 15 minutes

Participant Resource Guide Page Number: 63

Instructor's Notes

Learning Exercise: Riddle Me This...

Goal:

This exercise is designed to develop critical thinking and listening skills.

Materials:

The page entitled "Riddle Me This..." which can be found in the participant's Resource Guide page 64.

Approximate Time:

30 minutes

Instructions:

Participants will attempt to answer the 10 riddles. They are allowed to ask questions about the riddles and have them repeated.

Learning Exercise: Riddle Me This...

Using your listening and questioning skills try to
guess the answers to the riddles:

What gets wetter and wetter the more it dries?
A towel

You remove the outside and cook the inside. Then you eat the outside and throw away
the inside. What did you eat?
An ear of corn or a chicken

What can go around the world but stays in a corner?
A stamp

I have holes in my top and bottom, my left and right, and in the middle. But I still hold
water. What am I?
A sponge

Give me food, and I will live; give me water, and I will die. What am I?
Fire

The man who invented it doesn't want it. The man who bought it doesn't need it. The
man who needs it doesn't know it. What is it?
A coffin

Throw me off the highest building and I will not fall apart. But put me in the ocean and I
will. What am I?
A tissue

What can run but never walks, has a mouth but never talks, has a head but never weeps,
has a bed but never sleeps?
A river

No sooner spoken than broken. What is it?
Silence

Chapter 4

Creating Rapport
Instructor's Guide

Creating Rapport is divided into 2 learning modules each with multiple sections. Each module includes a quiz which reviews its learning objectives.

Learning to establish and maintain rapport with a wide variety of people will provide you with a strong foundation for customer service excellence.

Learning Objectives

Chapter 4 - Module 1

At the end of this module participants will be able to:

- Identify nonverbal communication.

- Empathize with and direct a customer who is upset.

- Apply rapport-building skills.

- Understand the importance of recognizing and responding to cultural differences.

Participant Resource Guide Page Number: 65

The Three Circles of Customer Service Success

Chapter 4 Rapport Skills reviews some of the skill sets required for managing the customer. This is one of The Three Circles of CS Success that you must understand to be effective as a customer service provider.

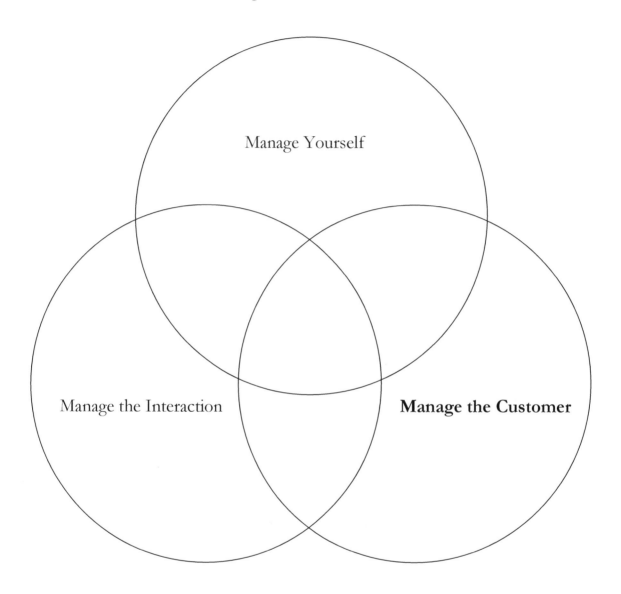

Manage the Customer

Creating rapport is related to managing the customer. To be effective you must:

- Understand how to interpret and react to someone's behavior.
- Guide the customer exchange to its successful conclusion.

Instructor's Notes

Nonverbal Communication

- Mehrabian, Wiener and Ferris' research at UCLA in 1967 determined that people principally rely on nonverbal communication to understand each other.

- Without seeing a person's nonverbal communication, such as body language and eye contact, it is easier to misunderstand the intent of their message.

- Some possible answers to the question "What are some examples of nonverbal communication you've seen at your facility?":
    o Arms folded/legs crossed – cautious/nervous
    o Lips pursed - angry
    o Squinting – trouble seeing/understanding
    o Foot tapping - impatient
    o Looking around/not making eye contact - uninterested

Approximate Time: 15 minutes

Participant Resource Guide Page Number: 67

Nonverbal Communication

Rapport occurs when people understand each other's feelings, communicate well and share a mutual trust.

In developing that understanding we rely more on nonverbal communication -- such as eye contact, posture and hand movement – than on just the spoken word.

Why? Because when we are unsure about what a person is saying it's in our nature to pay more attention to how they are saying it -- especially when they are upset.

What are some examples of nonverbal communication you've seen at your facility?

_____

_____

_____

_____

Instructor's Notes

Responding to an Emotional Customer

- Lead a discussion on the importance of appropriately responding to a customer's emotions in order to develop rapport with them.

- Describe the rule of empathize, then direct. This means that one shows empathy for the customer's situation then directs the conversation to the issue needing attention.

Approximate Time: 15 minutes

Participant Resource Guide Page Number: 68

Responding to an Emotional Customer

When responding to an emotional customer you should empathize with them then direct the conversation to the issue needing attention.

Empathy maintains rapport with the customer by letting them know you understand what they are feeling.

When responding to an emotional customer you should…

Reinforce positive aspects of the conversation:

- "I am pleased to hear…"   "You should feel good about…"

Show empathy for negative situations:

- "That must be frustrating…"   "I can understand how you feel…"

Apologize when you have inconvenienced the customer in some way:

- "I'm sorry about that..."   "That was my mistake..."

Instructor's Notes

Opportunities to Build Rapport

- Lead a discussion on taking advantage of opportunities to connect with customers and build rapport.

Approximate Time: 15 minutes

Participant Resource Guide Page Number: 69

Opportunities to Build Rapport

Want to boost your rapport building skills today?

Here are a few examples of how to improve relationships with the people at your facility:

- When first meeting new residents and their families shake hands and offer a warm greeting like: "I'm Camille, a nurse's aide. It's very nice to meet you."
- Walk family members to your facility's entrance to say good-bye just as you would at your own home.
  Ask a co-worker if you may help them with a task. They will often thank you and complete it themselves, but the rapport you've built is valuable to both of you.

Instructor's Notes

Cultural Differences Create Unique Challenges

- Lead a discussion about the importance of changing one's attitudes and behaviors in order to accommodate different cultures in at your facility.

- A staff member has to first identify the cultural difference then learn how to adjust by accepting rather than judging. Doing so will allow them to be more effective as a Customer Service Provider.

Approximate Time: 15 minutes

Participant Resource Guide Page Number: 70

Cultural Differences Create Unique Challenges

One of the greatest challenges in learning to develop rapport is taking into account the many cultural differences that exist within your facility.

Let's say you're a Caucasian CNA who recently began working at a facility where there are many residents and caregivers who are Asian.

You notice that the Asian residents and their families are reluctant to complain about things other residents might. This may sound like a good idea but it amounts to important information not being shared that could benefit the resident.

After questioning your colleagues you learn that privacy is very important to Asian families. Sharing feelings and personal information outside of the family circle is taboo because complaining is not considered dignified.

You decide that taking the time to gain the family's trust will make them more comfortable sharing information with you. And you reassure them that doing so "means better care for your loves ones."

What cultural differences do you observe at your facility? What adjustments to your behavior can you make when interacting with people from a culture different than yours?

_____

_____

_____

_____

Quiz Questions

Chapter 4 - Module 1

1. Rapport occurs when people understand each other's *feelings, communicate well and share a mutual trust.*

2. What are some appropriate comments to use when trying show empathy for negative situations?

   - *"That must be frustrating…"*
   - *"I can understand how you feel…"*

3. Describe a way that you can build rapport with a co-worker.

   - *Answers can include offering to help them, saying good morning, asking how their day is going, etc.*

4. List two ways that some of your co-workers' or residents' cultures are different than yours.

   - *Answers can include eating habits, dress, mannerisms, demeanor, etc.*

5. Why is it important to change your attitude and behavior about others by accepting, not judging, cultural differences?

   - *Answers can include gaining a better understanding of those I serve, making me a more effective communicator, making the residents' lives at our facility more enjoyable, etc.*

Approximate Time: 15 minutes

Participant Resource Guide Page Number: 71

Learning Objectives

Chapter 4 - Module 2

At the end of this module participants will be able to:

- Understand the Elements of Effective Communication.

- Appreciate the importance of being "on stage" as a customer service provider.

- Recognize opportunities to create "Customer Experiences".

Participant Resource Guide Page Number: 72

Instructor's Notes

The Elements of Effective Communication

- Describe and discuss the four elements of effective communication and how these elements are connected.

- Emphasize that one of the goals of customer service training is to help participants improve their communication skills which will increase their chances for success on the job and in life.

- Regarding the question "Even with your prompting some residents will not complain, choosing instead to suffer quietly. How will you encourage them to open up?"

    o Answers can include empathizing with residents by saying that sometimes it is uncomfortable to talk about being in pain or not feeling well; stating that sometimes you (as the caregiver) don't feel well and will say everything's OK when you really just want someone to comfort you.

Approximate Time: 15 minutes

Participant Resource Guide Page Number: 73

Elements of Effective Communication

Building rapport with someone requires that you communicate with them effectively. You must:

Picture your goal	The clearer that you imagine the outcome of a customer exchange, the more likely it will occur.
Manage your attitude	Your ability to manage your attitude will increase the chances that you'll achieve your service goal.
Pay attention	You must be attentive to the person you're speaking with in order to fully understand their message.
Be flexible	Adjust your behavior based on the person you are speaking with in order to improve rapport.

Interacting with the elderly requires some extra effort in order to understand and be understood...

Speak clearly and slowly while using common words.	Hold a resident's hands when you want to emphasize something.
Face the resident and smile while making eye contact.	Point to objects when speaking with the hearing impaired.

Even with your prompting some residents will not complain, choosing instead to suffer quietly. How will you encourage them to open up?

_____

_____

_____

Instructor's Notes

You Are a Performer So Play Your Part

- After participants read the story, lead a discussion about being "on stage". What does it mean to them?

- Ask participants if they've ever had an experience like Marisa's. Should the administrator reprimand her?

Approximate Time: 15 minutes

Participant Resource Guide Page Number: 74

You Are a Performer So Play Your Part

As a professional caregiver you are also playing the "role" of a customer service provider. This doesn't mean you are pretending to care about the people around you. It means when you put on your uniform you represent your community and your profession and you should act the part.

Sometimes you don't even need to be at your facility to make an impression about it...

Marisa is a CNA at a home in Minneapolis. She was running late for work and still had to bring her daughter to school. It was January and snowing. The unplowed roads were getting slicker by the minute.

After Marisa dropped off her daughter she pulled into a gas station around the corner from her nursing facility. As she filled her tank a homeless man asked her for some change. Instead of just refusing, she loudly criticized him for not working and "being lazy". The man walked away mumbling.

Marisa ran into work 15 minutes late and jumped into her rounds. An hour later, she passed by the administrator speaking with a visitor on tour in front of the building. The administrator introduced Marisa as a "top performing staff member" to the middle-aged gentleman.

After their brief meeting Marisa went back to work only to receive a call from the administrator shortly after asking her to come to the office.

Apparently the gentleman was not interested in having his father live at the home because of something Marisa had said. "Really? "I only asked him how old his father was and wished him a nice day." The administrator advised her: "No, Marisa, he was disappointed by something else. Apparently he was putting gas in his car this morning and overheard you shouting..."

When do you think you should be "on stage" as a customer service provider? When you step through the door at work? Only while on your shift? Whenever you wear your uniform in public?

_____

_____

_____

_____

Instructor's Notes

Creating a Customer Experience

- Lead a discussion about "customer experiences" participants have enjoyed. What made it an experience versus just good customer service?

- Discuss the different ways your community currently creates "customer experiences".

- Ask participants what new ideas they can come up with to provide their customers with an "experience".

Approximate Time: 15 minutes

Participant Resource Guide Page Number: 75

Creating a Customer Experience

In Chapter 1 we discussed customer touchpoints. Each time you interact with a customer you impact how they perceive the service you provide.

A customer experience is similar to a touchpoint but goes deeper. An example might be asking family members about a resident's special likes or dislikes then acting on that information. You might prepare a new resident's room with fresh flowers, a snack they enjoy or a handwritten note welcoming them.

When you create customer experiences, whether for residents or co-workers, the benefits are numerous: less friction, more cooperation and less stress.

What is one thing you can do today to go beyond delivering customer service to creating a customer experience?

_____

_____

_____

Quiz Questions

Chapter 4 - Module 2

1. What are the Elements of Effective Communication?

    a. *Picture your goal*
    b. *Manage your attitude*
    c. *Pay attention*
    d. *Be flexible*

2. Why is it important to recognize you are "on stage" as a customer service provider?

    Answers may include: It will help me to be aware that I represent myself, my community and profession; it will allow me to gain some perspective about my behavior which might help me rise above when I feel tired or stressed.

3. When should you consider yourself "on stage"?

    Whenever I where my uniform, name badge or other items that identify me as a professional at my facility.

4. What does it mean to deliver a "customer experience"?

    A customer experience is something that a customer service provider creates which encourages a customer to feel a positive connection to the CSP and their organization.

5. What are some things you can do to create a "customer experience"?

    Answers may include asking a resident to share stories about their life; completing a task for a co-worker unasked; buying something for a resident they cannot get at the facility; etc.

Approximate Time: 15 minutes

Participant Resource Guide Page Number: 76

Chapter 5

Managing Stress
Instructor's Guide

Managing Stress is divided into 3 learning modules each with multiple sections. Each module includes a quiz which reviews its learning objectives. Learning exercises can be found throughout the chapter.

**Being aware of what triggers stress
is the first step toward managing it.**

Learning Objectives

Chapter 5 - Module 1

At the end of this module participants will be able to:

- Understand the impact of stress on mind and body.

- Describe the stress response.

Participant Resource Guide Page Number: 77

Chapter 5 Managing Stress reviews some of the skill sets required for managing yourself. This is one of The Three Circles of CS Success that you must understand to be effective as a customer service provider.

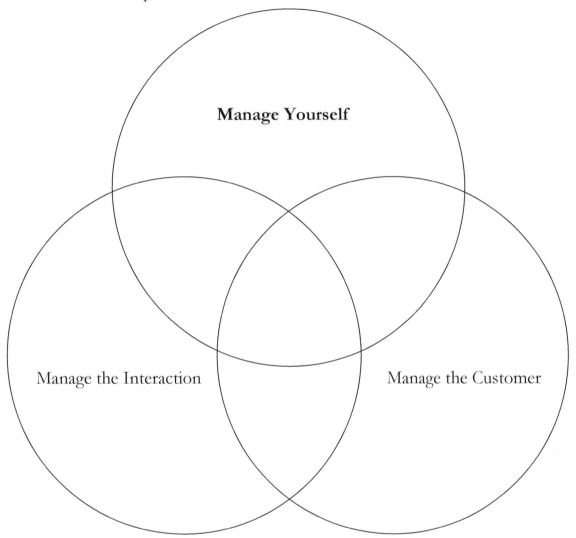

Manage Yourself

To effectively manage stress you must:

- Know how stress impacts you.
- Learn to detect your own stress signals.
- Use deep breathing and visualization techniques.

Participant Resource Guide Page Number: 78

Instructor's Notes

The Impact of Stress

- Discuss the nature and sources of stress.

- Ask participants to identify some examples of stressors that fit into each of the categories.

Approximate Time: 15 minutes

Participant Resource Guide Page Number: 79

The Impact of Stress

You will never be able to manage the customer better than you manage yourself

Three Sources of Stress

The environment	Your thoughts & emotions	Your physiology
External stressors can include the weather, traffic and noise. We often have little or no control over these outside sources of stress.	Examples can include visualizing a tragedy when someone is late or criticizing yourself harshly.	Illness, injury and discomforts like headaches can cause stress.

Stressors are often connected.

For example:

An environmental trigger such as being stuck in traffic...

Can create negative thoughts and emotions like imagining being late, creating justifications and feeling anxious...

These in turn can affect your physiology. Your muscles tense resulting in headaches and stomach upset.

The Alarm Response

- Explain the basic physiology of the alarm response. Note that it is a natural mechanism and serves the purpose of mobilizing a person's physical resources to deal with a threat.

- Describe how the response works in animals: they are able to shift out of the alarm response and return to normal within a short period of time. People tend to sustain the alarm response long after a threat has passed as well as through reliving an incident or through imagined threats.

- Explain that a sustained alarm response contributes to illnesses such as:

   o Cardiovascular diseases

   o Gastro-intestinal problems

   o Auto-immune diseases

Approximate Time: 15 minutes

Participant Resource Guide Page Number: 80

The Alarm Response

The alarm response is a series of biochemical changes that prepare you to deal with a perceived threat.

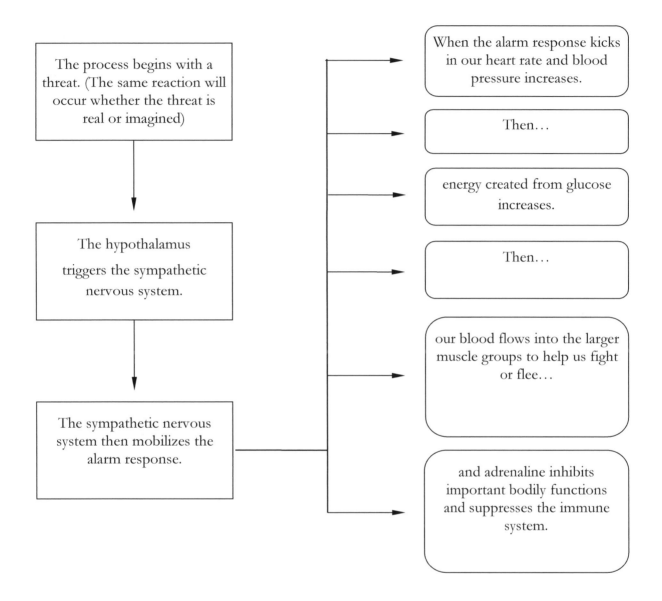

The alarm response is useful in situations where there is a real threat.

However, some people tend to maintain their alarm response for extended periods which can have damaging effects on the mind and body.

Chapter 5 - Module 1

1. What are three methods of managing stress?

   a. Know how stress impacts you

   b. Learn to detect your own stress signals

   c. Use deep breathing and visualization techniques

2. What are some examples of stressors created by:

   a. Your environment?

   - *External stressors can include the weather, traffic and noise.*

   b. Your thoughts and emotions?

   - *Mental images (visualizing a tragedy when someone is late) and internal dialogue (criticizing yourself harshly).*

   c. Your physiology?

   - *Illness, injury and discomforts such as headache or muscle tension.*

3. Does a threat need to be real or imagined to trigger the alarm response?

   - *Both real and imagined threats can trigger the alarm response.*

Approximate Time: 15 minutes

Participant Resource Guide Page Number: 81

Learning Objectives

Chapter 5 - Module 2

At the end of this module participants will be able to:

- Explain the role of perception in creating the stress response.
- Use reactive and proactive approaches to managing stress.

Participant Resource Guide Page Number: 82

Instructor's Notes

Stress and Perception

- Facilitate a discussion on the role perception plays in creating stress. Note how two people can respond differently to the same stressor.

Approximate Time: 15 minutes

Participant Resource Guide Page Number: 83

Stress and Perception

Researchers agree that it is not the triggering event that causes the alarm response, but the meaning that we place *on* the event. For example:

The Stimulus	Your Interpretation	You Respond with…
Your administrator scowls at you.	He thinks I am doing a bad job.	Anxiety - which is likely to produce the alarm response.
	Let's look at this situation again, but with a different interpretation.	
Your administrator scowls at you.	You think he must be tired or preoccupied.	Empathy

Instructor's Notes

Two Approaches to Stress Management

- Facilitate a discussion on the difference between a reactive approach and a proactive approach. A comprehensive plan to manage stress includes using coping skills from both approaches.

- One possible answer to the question "Name another reactive approach to reducing stress" may include asking the person to repeat themselves to make sure you understood their meaning while giving you a chance to pause before reacting.

- One possible answer to the question "Name another proactive approach to reducing stress" may include preparing yourself mentally before your shift with the thought that you are in control and do not have to overreact to stressors.

Approximate Time: 15 minutes

Participant Resource Guide Page Number: 84

Two Approaches to Stress Management

When we're *reactive* to stress we try to reduce its impact once it's occurred.

You can:

Change your environment -- just walking away from the stressful situation can have immediate benefits.

OR...

Change your response to the stressor -- try taking deep breaths and counting to 10 instead of yelling.

Name another reactive approach to reducing stress:

_____

_____

Being *proactive* means you change your *perspective* about the stressor.

For example, instead of reacting angrily at a co-worker for not helping you assist a resident, you might consider that they may be struggling with a difficult situation of their own.

Think of the benefits of being proactive and changing your perspective in this way:

It's like resetting the thermostat on a heater. If it is always set to go off at 88 degrees, it will probably run the whole winter. If it is *reset* for 68 degrees, it will run less often and conserve energy.

Name another proactive approach to reducing stress:

_____

_____

Both the reactive and proactive approaches can be practiced together since they complement each other.

Quiz Questions

Chapter 5 - Module 2

1. It is not the *triggering* event that causes the alarm response, but the *meaning* that we place on the event.

2. What are the two approaches to managing stress?

   - *The Reactive Approach and the Proactive Approach.*

3. Give an example of each of the two approaches.

   - *Reactive - taking deep breaths and counting to 10 instead of yelling.*

   - *Proactive - Instead of reacting angrily at a co-worker for not helping you assist a resident, you might consider that they may be struggling with a difficult situation of their own.*

Approximate Time: 15 minutes

Participant Resource Guide Page Number: 85

Learning Objectives

Chapter 5 - Module 3

At the end of this module participants will be able to:

- Use deep breathing to relax the mind and body.

- Practice visualization to remain calm.

Participant Resource Guide Page Number: 86

Instructor's Notes

Deep Breathing Exercise

- Point out that infants naturally breathe deeply into the abdomen and the lower part of the lungs. Adults tend to breathe into the lower lungs when we are deeply relaxed. Note that as few as two to four deep abdominal breaths will lower blood pressure, slow the heart rate and relax tight muscles.

- Guide the participants to practice abdominal breathing by placing one hand on their chest and one hand on their abdomen. The goal is to breathe slowly and deeply into the lower lungs so that the hand on the abdomen is moved outward first.

- Deep Breathing Exercise - continue guiding the participants through the breathing exercise adding the following elements:
  - o Start with deep, abdominal breathing as above. Add the idea of a whole body breath as if breathing in through the bottom of the feet and bringing the beneficial oxygen up into the whole body.

Approximate Time: 15 minutes

Participant Resource Guide Page Number: 87

Deep Breathing Exercise

Oxygen is brain food. This is why we use the term "brain dead" when someone is deprived of oxygen for a long time (or has just worked a double).

How we breathe impacts our emotional and mental states.

We tend to breathe in short, shallow breaths when tense. This limits the amount of nourishing oxygen to the brain and increases our discomfort.

Deep breathing forces more oxygen into the bloodstream. This releases endorphins which have a tranquilizing effect that promotes calmness.

Deep Breathing Exercise

Deep breathing for just two to three minutes has been found to help the mind and body relax. Try this exercise:

- **Break into a smile.** The idea is to get the facial muscles out of a grim or neutral position.

- **Slowly take a deep breath, hold if for 3 seconds, then slowly exhale.** Be sure to focus on abdominal breathing.

- **Make a silent, positive command such as "Mind Alert – Body Calm."** Begin this phrase at the peak of the inhale and finish it as you exhale.

- **Let your jaw and shoulders relax as you exhale.**

Visualization Exercise

- Discuss the power of visualization by revealing to participants how our mental images affect us. Explain that we can use this power to our advantage by visualizing positive outcomes and picturing success.

Approximate Time: 15 minutes

Participant Resource Guide Page Number: 88

Visualization Exercise

Your subconscious mind does not 'think' primarily in words. It is impacted more by images for the same reason that a picture is *worth* a thousand words.

It's more important to *show* yourself what you want than it is to *tell* yourself.

In this exercise you'll practice visualizing calmness.

1. **First, allow yourself to relax by taking three to five deep breaths.**

2. **When you are relaxed, close your eyes and imagine you are sitting comfortably in a movie theater looking at the screen.**

3. **Imagine a detailed picture of a quiet, relaxing scene on the screen.**

4. **Now see yourself climbing into the scene. You are no longer a spectator but are using all five senses to experience the relaxing environment around you.**

5. **Take these feelings with you as you open your eyes.**

Instructor's Notes

Learning Exercise: Bliss List

Goal:

    Provide participants the opportunity to consider what makes them happy.

Materials:

    Bliss List worksheet found in the participant's Resource Guide on page 89.

Approximate Time:

    30 minutes

Instructions:

- The Bliss List is a tool for considering the joys and blessings of life. The goal of the Bliss List is to engage in activities that bring happiness on a regular basis. Doing so helps to balance the tough times and brings more passion to life.

- Guide the participants through an exercise of listing activities, events or thoughts that bring joy into their lives. The objective is to fill at least one column on the page. If necessary, give examples along the way.

- It may be useful to have participants share some of the items on their Bliss List to inspire others.

Learning Exercise: Bliss List

One of the most powerful methods of reducing stress is to engage regularly in activities that you find relaxing, rewarding and enjoyable. Using the spaces below, create a list of these activities and post your Bliss List in at least three places where you will see it regularly. When you think of other enjoyable activities be sure to update your list.

_____   _____

_____   _____

_____   _____

_____   _____

_____   _____

_____   _____

_____   _____

_____   _____

_____   _____

_____   _____

I hereby commit to posting copies of my Bliss List in at least three places with the intention of reminding myself to enjoy as many of these activities as possible.

_____

Signature

Chapter 5 - Module 3

1. How does breathing impact our emotional and mental states?

- _Deep breathing forces more oxygen into the bloodstream. This releases endorphins which have a tranquilizing effect that promotes calmness._

2. It is more important to _show_ yourself what you want than it is to _tell_ yourself.

Approximate Time: 5 minutes

Participant Resource Guide Page Number: 90

Chapter 6

Resolving Conflict
Instructor's Guide

Resolving Conflict is divided into 4 learning modules each with multiple sections. Each module includes a quiz which reviews its learning objectives. A learning exercise can be found at the end of the chapter.

Working closely with colleagues and residents in a stressful environment will often lead to interpersonal challenges.

Learning Objectives

Chapter 6 - Module 1

At the end of this module participants will be able to:

- Understand the difference between negative and positive conflict.

- Identify which of the 5 Styles of Handling Conflict best reflects their personality.

- Recognize the impact of assuming both the best and the worst in a conflict.

Participant Resource Guide Page Number: 91

Chapter 6 Resolving Conflict reviews some of the skill sets required for managing yourself. This is one of The Three Circles of CS Success that you must understand to be effective as a customer service provider.

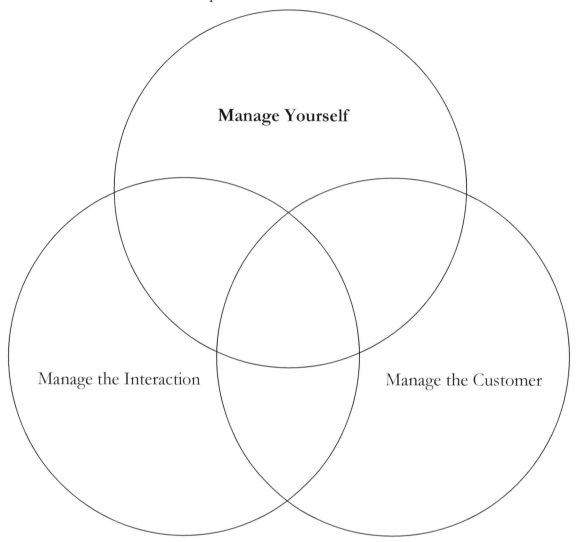

Manage Yourself

Relative to resolving conflict you manage yourself by:

- Keeping calm in the midst of conflict.

- Focusing on conflict resolution, not your position.

Participant Resource Guide Page Number: 92

Instructor's Notes

Understanding Conflict

- Lead a discussion on the nature of conflict and how conflict may be positive or negative.

- Note that self-serving behavior results in negative conflict and a lack of resolution.

Approximate Time: 15 minutes

Participant Resource Guide Page Number: 93

Understanding Conflict

Not all conflict is negative.

When both parties are to committed to overcoming differences and improving understanding conflicts can be resolved positively resulting in stronger relationships.

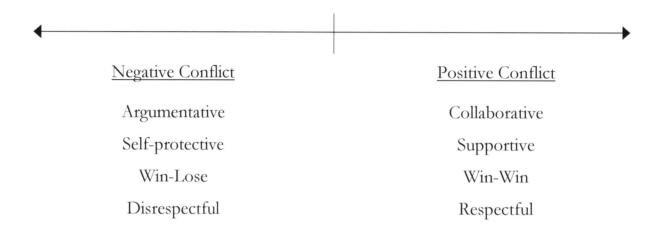

Negative Conflict

Argumentative

Self-protective

Win-Lose

Disrespectful

Positive Conflict

Collaborative

Supportive

Win-Win

Respectful

Understanding the styles people adopt to deal with conflict will increase the chances of resolving one.

The yin/yang symbol represents conflict because the nature of yin/yang lies in the interaction of two opposites.

Each side of a conflict contains some relationship to the other.

5 Styles of Handling Conflict

- Lead a discussion on the different methods people use to deal with conflict noting the pros and cons for each.

- Note that individuals often combine or switch methods. For example, an avoider may change tactics and become an aggressor.

Approximate Time: 15 minutes

Participant Resource Guide Page Number: 94

Accommodators put relationships first, ignore the issues and try to keep peace at any price.

Compromisers try to find fast, mutually acceptable solutions to a conflict that partially satisfies both parties.

Aggressors deal with conflict by arguing, being disrespectful or pulling rank.

Collaborators explore the disagreement from both sides, learn from each party's insights and creatively develop solutions that address everyone's concerns.

Avoiders may diplomatically postpone discussion or withdraw from a threatening situation.

Most people use a mix of styles. For example, an aggressor may decide at the end of a discussion that compromise is the best solution.

Which of these styles do you think best reflects your method of dealing with conflict? Why?

_____

_____

Instructor's Notes

Assuming the Worst in a Conflict

- Discuss the diagram which is based on the premise that someone is behaving with the intention to hurt another.

- Potential answers to the question "How would you turn this negative cycle into a 'win-win'?" may include:

    o Believing the other person is not trying to cause harm.

    o Asking questions to better understand the other party's behavior.

Approximate Time: 15 minutes

Participant Resource Guide Page Number: 95

Assuming the Worst in a Conflict

Many conflicts are maintained through a cycle which begins with assuming the other person is trying to take advantage of you. For example:

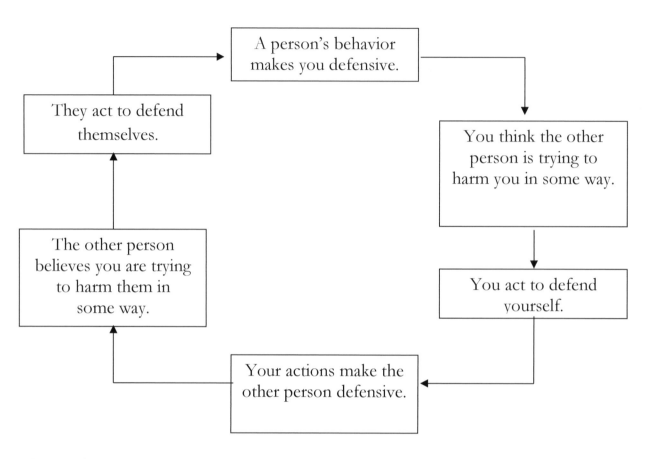

This cycle can escalate until one party is "defeated". In other words it is a win-lose situation.

How would you turn this cycle into a "win-win"?

_____

_____

_____

_____

Instructor's Notes

Assuming the Best in a Conflict

- Discuss why it's important to identify the positive intention behind another person's behavior. This is the assumption that people act with the intention of getting something positive for themselves, usually not to hurt someone.

- Assuming the best can establish mutual trust so the parties in a conflict can work toward a solution.

Approximate Time: 15 minutes

Participant Resource Guide Page Number: 96

Assuming the Best in a Conflict

When you assume the best in a conflict you believe that the other person is attempting to gain something without intentionally trying to hurt you.

In most cases assuming the worst provokes defensiveness, assuming the best supports openness.

- When assuming the best in a conflict you must **consider the circumstances from the other person's perspective.** We are often too caught up in our own point of view to consider another.

- **Try to soften your tone towards the other party.** Recognizing the other person's similarities to you promotes understanding.

- **Ask questions and start a conversation.** Doing so will help you better understand the other party's position.

When both people believe that the other is not trying to take something from them, trust can be established and the conflict likely resolved.

Quiz Questions

Chapter 6 - Module 1

1. List four characteristics each of negative conflict and positive conflict.

<u>Negative Conflict</u>	<u>Positive Conflict</u>
Argumentative	*Collaborative*
Self-protective	*Supportive*
Win-Lose	*Win-Win*
Disrespectful	*Respectful*

2. List the 5 styles used to deal with conflict. People can be…

   a. *Accommodators*

   b. *Compromisers*

   c. *Aggressors*

   d. *Collaborators*

   e. *Avoiders*

3. What does it mean when people "assume the worst" in a conflict?

   • *One or both parties believe that the other is behaving with the intention of harming them.*

Approximate Time: 15 minutes

Participant Resource Guide Page Number: 97

Learning Objectives

Chapter 6 - Module 2

At the end of this module participants will be able to:

- Assert themselves respectfully.

- Explain the difference between being "Problem Focused" and "Solution Focused".

- Avoid most conflicts by following 4 simple steps.

Participant Resource Guide Page Number: 98

Instructor's Notes

Asserting Yourself

- A primary skill in dealing with conflict is to assert yourself while maintaining respect for others.

- Discuss the benefits of using "I" statements. Have participants practice creating "I" statements for wants, needs and for sharing opinions. Use this as an opportunity to practice active listening which requires that the listener feedback to the speaker what they've heard for confirmation or correction.

- For detailed information on active listening please review the Instructor's Guide Chapter 3 "Listening Skills" page 74.

Approximate Time: 15 minutes

Participant Resource Guide Page Numbers: 99-100

Asserting Yourself

A primary skill used in dealing with conflict is to assert yourself while maintaining respect for others.

There are three aspects of asserting yourself:

1. Making requests by clearly stating your wants and needs

- Communicating what you want can be accomplished through making "I" statements:
  - "I need undisturbed time to work on the report." NOT "You need to leave me alone."

2. Opening up by sharing feelings and opinions

- Discovering the similarities and differences between yourself and others develops understanding and trust.

- Your goal is to share your thoughts without forcing the other person to agree or implying their opinion is wrong.
  - You should use terms like...
    - I think...
    - I feel...
    - In my opinion...

3. Setting Boundaries

- Problems can be avoided when you're clear about what you want and what you don't want.
  - Sharing expectations about others behavior.
    - When sharing expectations, be honest and respectful: "It hurts my feeling when you shout at me. I'd like you to tell me what you want without yelling."
  - Telling others when they have crossed boundaries.

- We need to have personal boundaries and be clear what they are: "I don't like it when you eat the food I brought for lunch. Please stop doing that."

o Establishing consequences for crossing boundaries.

  - If you don't like it when a co-worker bad-mouths someone, you could say: "When you say negative things about Jennifer it bothers me because I like her. I won't talk to you if you do it in the future." If your co-worker says negative things about Jennifer again, walk away.

Instructor's Notes

Problem Focused vs. Solution Focused

- Lead a discussion on being problem focused in the context of conflict resolution. We look for what is wrong and then find who or what is to blame for it. This thinking tends to limit us because we are constantly finding sources, outside of ourselves, to blame for our troubles.

- Being problem focused leads to a belief that the world outside of us (a person, a situation) must change in order for us to be happy or to get what we want.

- Discuss what it means to be solution focused. This type of thinking is based on identifying what we want and holding ourselves accountable for achieving our goals.

Approximate Time: 15 minutes

Participant Resource Guide Page Number: 101

Problem Focused vs. Solution Focused

Your approach to resolving conflict will determine the outcome. You are either Problem Focused or Solution Focused:

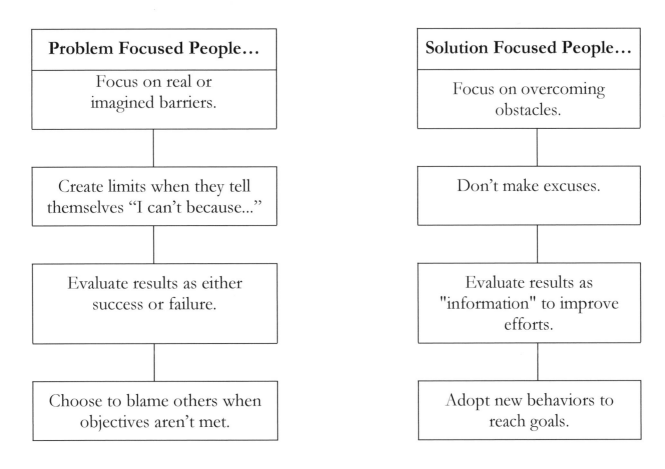

Problem Focused People...	Solution Focused People...
Focus on real or imagined barriers.	Focus on overcoming obstacles.
Create limits when they tell themselves "I can't because..."	Don't make excuses.
Evaluate results as either success or failure.	Evaluate results as "information" to improve efforts.
Choose to blame others when objectives aren't met.	Adopt new behaviors to reach goals.

Instructor's Notes

4 Steps to Avoid Conflict

- Lead a discussion about the 4 steps and how they relate to each other.

- Ask the participants if they have encountered a situation like the one at the bottom of the page. Did they also overreact based on their assumptions?

Approximate Time: 15 minutes

Participant Resource Guide Page Number: 102

4 Steps to Avoid Conflict

It is far better to avoid conflict than to deal with it. Here are some actions to take that will help you avoid conflict:

1. **Take ownership of your role in the conflict**

   - You need to recognize that you add to the problem by thinking you're "right" and the other person is "wrong". You express these thoughts through your opinions, judgments and actions.

2. **Don't make "You" statements**

   - "You" statements tend to blame the other person for the problem and put them on the defensive. For example: "You need to stop bothering me."

3. **Instead Make "I" statements when offering your opinion**

   - "I" statements describe a problem in terms of your feelings about a behavior, the behavior itself and the result of the behavior. "I get annoyed when you interrupt me because it breaks my concentration."

4. **Don't become defensive**

   - Defensiveness is a common response when you believe you're being attacked. Unfortunately this will make the other person defensive as well, killing rapport. Try not to take their behavior personally.

Consider This Scenario

A co-worker you've had a conflict with is staring at you as she heads your way. Judging from the look on her face she appears to be upset. **What are your first thoughts?**

The co-worker stops you and stiffly says "Wait a minute." **What are you thinking now?**

You respond by angrily asking her: "What's your problem!'

Her tone changes when she tells you that her daughter fell off the swings at school and hurt her arm. She asks if you can stay late to finish up for her since she has to leave immediately.

What do you think caused your reaction? Your assumptions? Your defensiveness?

_____

_____

Quiz Questions

Chapter 6 - Module 2

1. What are three examples of asserting yourself?

    a. Making requests by clearly stating your wants and needs

    b. Opening up by sharing feelings and opinions

    c. Setting boundaries

2. Being <u>*Problem*</u> Focused means you concentrate on real or imagined barriers and how they are limiting you. Being <u>*Solution*</u> Focused means you are directed toward a desired goal and will find ways to overcome obstacles so you can achieve it.

3. What are the 4 Steps to Avoid Conflict?

    a. Take ownership of your role in the conflict

    b. Don't make "You" statements

    c. Make "I" statements when offering your opinion

    d. Don't become defensive

4. What is an "I" statement?

    "I" statements describe a problem in terms of your feelings about a behavior, the behavior itself and the result of the behavior. For example: "I get annoyed when you interrupt me because it breaks my concentration."

Approximate Time: 15 minutes

Participant Resource Guide Page Number: 103

Learning Objectives

Chapter 6 - Module 3

At the end of this module participants will be able to:

- Apply the steps commonly used to resolve conflicts.

- Use an effective technique to overcome intercultural conflicts.

Participant Resource Guide Page Number: 104

Instructor's Notes

Steps for Resolving Conflict: Part 1 - The Preparation

- Review and discuss Steps 1-6 for resolving conflicts.

- Stress the importance of writing down the main points to be discussed using non-threatening language before meeting with the other party. This will keep the discussion on track and avoid creating more conflict.

- Mediation is a specialized skill which requires training. If a mediator is required to resolve a conflict both parties should allow adequate time to agree upon one.

Approximate Time: 15 minutes

Participant Resource Guide Page Numbers: 105-106

Steps for Resolving Conflict
Part 1 - The Preparation

You probably experience or witness some kind of conflict every day at your facility. It occurs between:

- Co-workers
- Managers and employees
- Staff and residents
- Between the residents themselves

Although there are no easy formulas for resolving conflict there are some basic steps that you can follow to get started in the right direction.

<u>Steps for Resolving Conflict: Part 1 - The Preparation</u>

When preparing to resolve a conflict focus on finding a win-win solution, not just a "win" for yourself.

1. **Discover the other party's motivation to resolve the conflict.** If you are truly interested in ending the conflict then ask the other party if they are, too.

2. **Set your goals.** Take the time to become clear about what you want by outlining, in writing, what your hoped-for outcomes are.

3. **Plan what you are going to discuss.** Write out your main points in non-threatening language. This will help keep the discussion on track and avoid creating more conflict.

4. **Determine the time and place to talk.** Both parties should agree on a neutral space free of interruptions and distractions.

5. **Agree on some guidelines**.

   - **Do not make or accept threats.** This only serves to create hostility and reduce trust.

   - **Don't give up even if you are both frustrated.** It's OK to take a break but make a commitment to find an acceptable solution.

   - **Stick to the issues.** Remember to focus the discussion on the issues which created the problem. Don't dig up old conflicts.

6. **Find a mediator to guide the discussion, if necessary.** If you or the other person feels uncomfortable with each other invite an unbiased party to keep things moving forward.

Think of a conflict you currently have with someone at your facility. Using the steps outlined on the preceding page, answer the questions below detailing how you will work through your issues.

Conflict Resolution Plan

I am having a conflict with _____

about_____

1. How would you like to see the conflict resolved?

_____

_____

2. What are the main points you will discuss with the other person?

_____

_____

3. Where and when will you suggest a meeting? Why did you choose this time and location?

_____

_____

4. How open do you think the other party will be to finding a solution? If you don't think they will want to cooperate what can you do to change their mind?

_____

_____

Approximate Time: 15 minutes

Participant Resource Guide Page Number: 107

Instructor's Notes

Steps for Resolving Conflict: Part 2 - The Meeting

- Refer to the benefits of using "I" statements for asserting one's feelings while trying to establish and maintain rapport with the other person. (See Chapter 6 Module 2 for more information)

- Stress the importance of trying to determine what the other person's intentions are at the beginning of the discussion by asking questions such as:

    o Why do you think we are in conflict?

    o What do you hope to gain from our discussion?

- Understanding what motivates each party will help them set the right expectations about resolving the conflict.

- Focus on shared interests, not individual positions. The parties in a conflict should identify what they want without getting stuck behind inflexible demands.

Approximate Time: 15 minutes

Participant Workbook Page Number: 108

Steps for Resolving Conflict
Part 2 - The Meeting

Once you and the other person meet you should follow these steps:

1. **Begin by expressing appreciation and optimism.** The fact that you are getting together is already a good sign that a solution is possible.

2. **Ask questions to get the other person to open up without interrupting or judging.** Start by asking them: "Why do you think we are in conflict?"

3. **Acknowledge the other person's feelings and opinions.** Practice active listening. Backtrack and summarize what you have heard to confirm you understand.

4. **Define the issues related to the conflict.** Collaborate to put the issues in writing.

5. **Set your goals for resolving the conflict.** Also list your expectations for working through the problem together. For example, you should both agree not to interrupt.

6. **Identify something that you both find important.** Consider the bigger picture: "Don't we just want to do our jobs and help our residents as best we can? Doesn't arguing get in the way of that?"

7. **Maintain responsibility for your feelings.** Use "I" statements to acknowledge opinions and feelings as your own.

8. **Work toward an agreement.** Focus on shared interests, not individual positions. Finding a mutually agreeable solution requires not getting stuck behind inflexible demands.

9. **If you get stuck try a different tactic.** When negotiations hit a roadblock try looking at the issue from a different angle. "Since you've been here longer why don't you suggest how we can get past this issue?" This approach plays to the other person's ego and is hard to resist.

10. **Create a plan for handling conflict in the future.** Agree how each of you will work toward future problem resolution.

As you did on the previous page consider a current conflict you are having at work. Step 10 above requires that you work together on a plan for handling future conflicts. **What will your suggestions be?**

_____

_____

_____

Instructor's Notes

Intercultural Conflict

- Review the story and facilitate a discussion about the intercultural differences found at your facility.

- Begin this discussion by asking participants: "What are some questions you have about the different cultures found in our facility?"

  o These questions should concentrate on general cultural differences and not be addressed to specific people. This exercise is not about finding fault, but gaining understanding.

  o Participants can use the bottom of page 109 in their Resource Guide to write down their questions.

- Stress to participants that this learning session is not the environment to point fingers at specific people. If co-workers wish to discuss a problem ask them to speak together after the session or refer them to management.

Approximate Time: 15 minutes

Participant Resource Guide Page Number: 109

Intercultural Conflict

When we disagree it's with someone who belongs to any number of groups based on gender, sexual orientation, age, nationality or race. And each one of these groups have a culture associated with it.

We can practice tolerance and gain understanding about different cultures when we use conflict as a learning opportunity.

A nursing home in San Francisco was experiencing challenges due to a clash of cultures.

Certain Caucasian staff members felt the Latino staff didn't speak up and often withdrew from heated discussions. And some of the Latino staffers felt their Caucasian colleagues were loud, pushy and aggressive.

Management suggested staff members should attempt to resolve their conflict by writing down questions concerning the differences between cultures.

The setting was more like a game show than a formal meeting. The questions were read by a manager and were answered by random representatives of the cultures present.

Some of the questions asked included:

- Why do you avoid dealing with an issue instead of confronting it?
- How come you harass me with complaints about how I do my job?
- Why do you embarrass me with questions in the staff meetings?

The exercise allowed participants to learn about each other and their cultures in a safe, productive environment. In doing so the participants also discovered the many similarities they share.

**List any questions you have about the different
cultures found at your facility.**

_____

_____

_____

_____

Quiz Questions

Chapter 6 - Module 3

1. What are the 6 steps to prepare for conflict resolution?

    a. *Discover the other party's motivation to resolve the conflict*

    b. *Set your goals*

    c. *Plan what you are going to discuss*

    d. *Determine the time and place to talk*

    e. *Agree on some guidelines*

    f. *Find a mediator to guide the discussion, if necessary*

2. What are the 10 steps to follow when meeting to discuss a conflict?

    a. *Begin by expressing appreciation and optimism*

    b. *Ask questions to get the other person to open up without interrupting or judging*

    c. *Acknowledge the other person's feelings and opinions*

    d. *Define the issues related to the conflict*

    e. *Set your goals for resolving the conflict*

    f. *Identify something that you both find important*

    g. *Maintain responsibility for your feelings*

    h. *Work toward an agreement*

    i. *If you get stuck try a different tactic*

    j. *Create a plan for handling conflict in the future*

Approximate Time: 15 minutes

Participant Resource Guide Page Number: 110

Learning Objectives

Chapter 6 - Module 4

At the end of this module participants will be able to:

- Avoid the negative impact of judging a customer.

- Identify 5 challenging customer types and their related behaviors.

- Manage an exchange with an abusive customer.

Participant Resource Guide Page Number: 111

Instructor's Notes

Judging Your Customers

- Discuss the difference between a person's behavior and the person. People have a tendency to characterize a person based on minimal information. A common example is thinking the bad driver ahead of you is an "idiot" for cutting you off rather than considering they may have just been distracted for a moment by the infant in their car.

- Stephen Covey, in *7 Habits of Highly Successful People,* tells the story about a father and his two young sons on a crowded Manhattan subway. The boys are rowdy: ripping papers out of passengers hands, stepping on feet and yelling while the father sits there staring into space. Finally a passenger scolds the man: "Why don't you do something about your kids!" The father wearily looks at the passenger and says "Oh, I'm sorry. We're going home from the hospital where their mother just passed away." Ask participants how they think the passenger's perception of the situation changed after hearing that. How do they think the passenger responded to the father?

Approximate Time: 15 minutes

Participant Resource Guide Page Number: 112

Judging Your Customers

People are quick to make judgments about others.

For example, it is easy to label a customer who incorrectly follows your directions as "stupid" rather than just being a little slow to comprehend due to illness, age, medication or some other factor.

When you pass judgment on your customers it...

...reduces your effectiveness as a Customer Service Provider.

- You may neglect some of your customer service skills because you believe they don't apply to someone who you've labeled negatively.

...encourages you to treat your customers as you perceive them.

- Your language and behavior toward the customer will be based on your negative judgment about them.

Empathy is the ability to understand and share the feelings of another.

At one time or another most of us have gotten upset when dealing with a customer service provider. Thinking of our own experiences as *a* customer will help us become more empathetic toward *our* customers.

Dealing with Challenging Customer Behaviors

- Discuss the behavior patterns listed which many Customer Service Providers will find difficult to work with.

- For each customer "label", ask the participants to fill in the common judgments that they would make about the customer. Some examples are listed below:

Challenging Customer "Label"	Common Judgment
Overconfident	• Aggressive • "Know-it-all" • Arrogant
Slow responder	• Stupid
Quiet	• Stupid • Uncooperative
Talkative	• Needy • Lonely • Burdensome
Distraught	• Needy • Demanding • Emotional

Approximate Time: 15 minutes

Participant Resource Guide Page Number: 113

Dealing with Challenging Customer Behaviors

In this exercise, you'll work with 5 behaviors that a Customer Service Provider will face. List the judgment you might make about the types of customers labeled.

Customer "Label"	Associated Behaviors	Your Judgment
Overconfident	Speaks with certainty Tends to interrupt Does not listen Tells you how to do your job Blames you or your facility	
Slow	Talks very slowly Asks you to repeat yourself Seems confused Gives long pauses after you ask a question	
Quiet	Offers short answers Does not engage in small talk Let's you take the initiative	
Talkative	Gives long-winded answers Strays into unrelated subjects Gives unnecessary details	
Distraught	Has emotional outbursts Details the "pain" the situation has "caused" them	

Instructor's Notes

Working with an Abusive Customer

- Facilitate a discussion on dealing with an abusive customer—a customer that is yelling, using profanity or making verbal threats.

- If your facility's policy requires ending a phone conversation with an abusive customer, suggest that participants warn the customer before hanging up.

- Point out the importance of managing oneself in abusive situations and that the Customer Service Provider should make an attempt to calm the person down before ending the interaction.

- Facilitate a role-play involving an abusive customer using the guidelines listed on the following page. Select a group member to play the Customer Service Provider while the instructor acts as the customer. If applicable, discuss your facility's guidelines for dealing with abusive customers first.

Approximate Time: 15 minutes

Participant Resource Guide Page Number: 114

Working with an Abusive Customer

On occasion some customers will resort to yelling, cursing or calling you names when they are angry or frustrated.

You are not obligated to accept insults or threats from a customer. But you should never become abusive yourself.

Abusive customers:

- Will often shout demands.

- May use profanity.

- May gesture aggressively.

Guidelines For Working With An Abusive Customer

When working with an abusive customer try to use the customer's name when attempting to calm them down. Personalizing the exchange may make the customer less likely to continue the abuse.

Advise, but do not threaten, the customer that you will end the conversation (hang up or walk away) if they continue to act inappropriately.

It Takes Two

While a customer's behavior may be challenging it is your

***response* to their behavior that can avoid - or create - a conflict.**

What judgments might you make about someone who is being abusive?

_____

_____

Quiz Questions

Chapter 6 - Module 4

1. What two things happen when you pass judgment on your customers?

    a. It reduces your effectiveness as a Customer Service Provider.

    b. It encourages you to treat the customer as you judge them.

2. What are 5 challenging customer types?

    a. Overconfident

    b. Slow

    c. Quiet

    d. Talkative

    e. Distraught

3. What should you do when working with an abusive customer?

    Use the customer's name when attempting to calm them down. If that doesn't work advise them, but do not threaten, that you will end the conversation (hang up or walk away) if they continue to act inappropriately.

Approximate Time: 15 minutes

Participant Resource Guide Page Number: 115

Instructor's Notes

Learning Exercise: Conflict Scenarios

Goal:

This role-play exercise teaches the importance of preparation and strategy in resolving conflict.

Materials:

The Conflict Scenarios worksheet included in the participant's Resource Guide on pages 116-117.

Approximate Time:

30 minutes

Instructions:

Break the participants into 5 groups. Each group will work with one of the challenging customer "labels". Each group selects one member to play the Customer Service Provider and one to play the customer. The group should come up with a role-play to demonstrate how the Customer Service Provider would manage their assigned "challenging" customer. Ask the participants to take turns playing each of the roles.

Learning Exercise: Conflict Scenarios

Scenario One

You have worked in a nursing facility for over six months. Last month an employee from a sister facility transferred in. The new employee, Margie, is sometimes bright and competent and at other times distracted and forgetful. She has severe mood swings going from cheerful to depressed in minutes. There are times when she harasses you and your co-workers. You have made an appointment with your supervisor to discuss the problem.

How will you open the conversation?

_____

_____

Scenario Two

You have a conflict with a resident, Mrs. Bell. You think she is inconsiderate because she talks loudly, speaks badly about others and demands things her way. You have been assigned to be her permanent caregiver.

How will you handle the situation?

_____

_____

Scenario Three

You have just received a poor rating from your DON, Chris. This seems unfair because you have worked very hard and have not received any warnings. You have made an appointment with Chris to discuss the issue.

What is your strategy for meeting with Chris? What outcome are you hoping for?

_____

_____

Scenario Four

You are having lunch with a co-worker. She casually mentions that she overheard another co-worker saying things about you that are untrue.

What will you do about the gossip?

_____

_____

Scenario Five

You are currently experiencing some personal problems which often upsets you at work, affecting your concentration. You have also had some attendance problems. You know that poor attendance and sloppy performance are cause for disciplinary action or even termination. You like your job and can't afford to lose it. Your supervisor has asked to see you in her office.

What are you assuming your supervisor wants to discuss? How will you prepare for the conversation?

_____

_____

Training Evaluation Survey

Your Name (optional):

_____

Facility Name:

_____

Workbook/Module/Section being evaluated:
(Example: Resolving Conflict/Module 2/Asserting Yourself)

_____

1. How much of today's training do you think will be useful on the job?

____ 25% ____ 50% ____75% ____ 100%

2. What other customer service related information would you like to see in future editions of this course?

_____

3. Overall, what would you rate your training experience today?
(Five being the best experience)

1   2   3   4   5

4. What could we have done to make your training experience more effective and worth your time?

_____

Participant Resource Guide Page Number: 118

ABOUT THE AUTHOR

Rob Anderson has been training and managing customer service organizations in both the public and private sectors for over 20 years. Bringing a fresh approach to customer service in Long Term Care, Rob has worked with facilities throughout the United States to develop easy-to-use training materials that improve the way frontline staff work with each other and with residents.

Made in the USA
Charleston, SC
27 May 2015